IN THEIR
OWN WORDS

IN THEIR
OWN WORDS

A History of
the American Negro

1619-1865

EDITED BY MILTON MELTZER

THOMAS Y. CROWELL COMPANY

NEW YORK

I wish to thank The Hampton Institute for permission to reprint the excerpts from the recollections of slavery which appear on pages 42-50 (these were originally published in *The Negro in Virginia,* copyright 1940 by The Hampton Institute) and the University of Chicago Press and Benjamin A. Botkin for the material on pages 174-181, which first appeared in *Lay My Burden Down,* copyright 1945 by the University of Chicago Press.

I wish to thank the following for permission to reproduce the illustrations on the pages indicated:

The Bettmann Archive, page 41; Connecticut Historical Society, page 75; New York Public Library, pages 17, 51, 89, 102, 118; Picture Collection of the New York Public Library, pages 1, 79, 145, 152, 173; Rare Book Collection of the New York Public Library, page 59; Schomburg Collection of the New York Public Library, page 126.
I should like, once again, to express my deep appreciation to Anne Coldewey for her help in the preparation of the manuscript.

Foreword

This book tries to help the reader understand what American Negroes felt, thought, did, suffered, and enjoyed down through that great divide in our history, the Civil War.

Because history is written so largely by the people who came out on top, the history books have little to say about the human cost of the past. In America, what happened to the Negro has been largely neglected by historians, or distorted, with honorable exceptions.

What the Negro has had done to him, how he has lived through it, and how he has fought back, is the living stuff of his history. In this book he tells the story in his own words—through letters, diaries, journals, autobiographies, speeches, resolutions, newspapers, pamphlets. These records reveal to us what happened to living men, women, and children of the past. But they also help us to see why things are the way they are today. Negroes today, as Langston Hughes put it, want "pay-

ment long overdue—since 1619." The young—and the old, too—want it now, before they grow too old and die without it, as did every generation now under ground.

The arrangement of the book proceeds from slavery to Emancipation and the close of the Civil War. With a vast amount of source material to draw upon, choices were made to show the life of the slave and the free Negro, and the struggle of both to win freedom, equal rights, and full citizenship, a struggle that still goes on more than a hundred years later. Subsequent volumes of In Their Own Words *will bring the story up to the present.*

There is a brief introduction to each document. Some of the documents are given in full; many have been shortened, but without changing their meaning. In some cases I have taken the liberty of paragraphing and of modernizing punctuation for the sake of easier reading. The source is given at the end of each document. The index and the reading list will be of additional help to the reader.

MILTON MELTZER

Contents

IN THEIR
OWN WORDS

A Dutch warship brought the first cargo of twenty Negroes to Virginia in 1619. Millions of other Negroes were torn from their African homes and carried to the New World before the slave trade was ended. The Africans brought here against their will were not born slaves. In their homeland they were free farmers and herdsmen, craftsmen skilled in pottery and weaving, woodcarving and ironworking. They were traders and hunters, musicians and dancers, poets and sculptors. Some were princes and warriors, rulers of kingdoms large and small.

In Africa their cultures were rich and varied, as different from one another as were the African peoples themselves. Their colors, their languages, their food, their clothing differed in a range as great as the difference in size between the pygmies and the giant Watusi of Africa.

They came in chains, brought by men who chose to use slaves because they would bring greater profits than the mas-

1

ters could get from their own labor, or from other types of labor.

The Negroes were no better fitted physically to do the hard labor of the agricultural South than were the whites. Nor were Negroes better fitted psychologically to live in slavery. In the past, it must be remembered, long before America was colonized, whites of many countries had been forced to submit to slavery. With the same variety of brains and emotions, the same range of ability and personality, Negroes could find slavery no more a blessing than could whites.

As traffic with the New World increased, and the demand for slave labor swelled, the buying and selling of Africans gave way to piracy and kidnapping.

Americans did not neglect the profits of the trade. By 1645 a Yankee sea captain was sailing the Rainbowe out of Boston on the first American voyage for slaves. Down to the War for Independence the slave trade was vital to New England's merchants.

An early victim of slave trading was Gustavus Vassa. He was born in Benin in 1745. At the age of eleven, he was kidnapped from his family and sold into slavery. Later he was sold again to traders and chained on a slave ship bound for America. He was sold to a Virginia planter, and then to a British naval officer, and finally to a Philadelphia merchant who gave him the chance to buy his freedom. As a ship's steward he travelled widely. He also worked to bring an end to the slave trade. In 1791, he wrote his autobiography. It contains a passage describing the voyage of the slave ship that carried him to America.

I saw a slave ship . . .
1760

THE FIRST OBJECT which saluted my eyes when I arrived on the coast was the sea, and a slave ship, which was then riding at anchor, and waiting for its cargo. These filled me with astonishment, which was soon connected with terror, when I was carried on board. I was immediately handled, and tossed up to see if I were sound, by some of the crew; and I was now persuaded that I had gotten into a world of bad spirits, and that they were going to kill me. Their complexions too differing so much from ours, their long hair, and the language they spoke (which was very different from any I had ever heard), united to confirm me in this belief.

Indeed, such were the horrors of my views and fears at the moment, that, if ten thousand worlds had been my own, I would have freely parted with them all to have exchanged my condition with that of the meanest slave in my own country. When I looked round the ship too and saw a large furnace or copper boiling, and a multitude of black people of every description chained together, every one of their countenances ex-

3

pressing dejection and sorrow, I no longer doubted of my fate; and, quite overpowered with horror and anguish, I fell motionless on the deck and fainted.

When I recovered a little, I found some black people about me, who I believed were some of those who had brought me on board, and had been receiving their pay; they talked to me in order to cheer me, but all in vain. I asked them if I were not to be eaten by those white men with horrible looks, red faces, and long hair. They told me I was not: and one of the crew brought me a small portion of spirituous liquor in a wine glass; but being afraid of him, I would not take it out of his hand. One of the blacks therefore took it from him and gave it to me, and I took a little down my palate, which, instead of reviving me, as they thought it would, threw me into the greatest consternation at the strange feeling it produced, having never tasted any such liquor before.

Soon after this, the blacks who brought me on board went off, and left me abandoned to despair. I now saw myself deprived of all chance of returning to my native country, or even the least glimpse of hope of gaining the shore, which I now considered as friendly; and I even wished for my former slavery in preference to my present situation, which was filled with horrors of every kind, still heightened by my ignorance of what I was to undergo.

I was not long suffered to indulge my grief; I was soon put down under the decks, and there I received such a salutation in my nostrils as I had never experienced in my life: so that with the loathsomeness of the stench and crying together, I became so sick and low that I was not able to eat, nor had I the least desire to taste anything.

4

I now wished for the last friend, death, to relieve me; but soon, to my grief, two of the white men offered me eatables; and, on my refusing to eat, one of them held me fast by the hands, and laid me across, I think, the windlass, and tied my feet, while the other flogged me severely.

I had never experienced anything of this kind before; and although, not being used to the water, I naturally feared that element the first time I saw it, yet nevertheless, could I have got over the nettings, I would have jumped over the side, but I could not; and, besides, the crew used to watch us very closely who were not chained down to the decks, lest we should leap into the water: and I have seen some of these poor African prisoners most severely cut for attempting to do so, and hourly whipped for not eating. This indeed was often the case with myself.

In a little time after, amongst the poor chained men, I found some of my own nation, which in a small degree gave ease to my mind. I inquired of these what was to be done with us? They gave me to understand we were to be carried to these white people's country to work for them. I then was a little revived, and thought, if it were no worse than working, my situation was not so desperate.

But still I feared I should be put to death, the white people looked and acted, as I thought, in so savage a manner; for I had never seen among any people such instances of brutal cruelty; and this not only shewn towards us blacks, but also to some of the whites themselves.

One white man in particular I saw, when we were permitted to be on deck, flogged so unmercifully with a large rope near the foremast, that he died in consequence of it; and they tossed him over the side as they would have done a brute. This made me fear these people the more; and I expected nothing less than to be treated in the same manner.

I could not help expressing my fears and apprehensions to some of my countrymen: I asked them if these people had no country, but lived in this hollow place (the ship)? They told me they did not, but came from a distant one.

"Then," said I, "how comes it in all our country we 'never heard of them!' " They told me because they lived so very far off. I then asked where were their women? Had they any like themselves? I was told they had: "And why," said I, "do we not see them?" They answered, because they were left behind.

I asked how the vessel could go? They told me they could not tell; but that there were cloth put upon the masts by the help of the ropes I saw, and then the vessel went on; and the white men had some spell or magic they put in the water when they liked in order to stop the vessel. I was exceedingly amazed at this account, and really thought they were spirits. I therefore wished much to be from amongst them, for I expected they would sacrifice me: but my wishes were vain; for we were so quartered that it was impossible for any of us to make our escape.

While we stayed on the coast I was mostly on deck; and one day, to my great astonishment, I saw one of these vessels coming in with the sails up. As soon as the whites saw it, they gave a great shout, at which we were amazed; and the more so as the vessel appeared larger by approaching nearer. At last she came to an anchor in my sight, and when the anchor was let go I and my countrymen who saw it were lost in astonishment to observe the vessel stop; and were now convinced it was done by magic.

Soon after this the other ship got her boats out, and they came on board of us, and the people of both ships seemed very glad to see each other. Several of the strangers also shook hands with us, black people, and made motions with their hands, signifying I suppose, we were to go to their country; but we did not understand them.

At last, when the ship we were in had got in all her cargo, they made ready with many fearful noises, and we were all put under deck, so that we could not see how they managed the vessel.

But this disappointment was the least of my sorrow. The stench of the hold while we were on the coast was so intolerably loathsome that it was dangerous to remain there for any time, and some of us had been permitted to stay on the deck for the fresh air; but now that the whole ship's cargo were confined together, it became absolutely pestilential.

The closeness of the place, and the heat of the climate, added to the number in the ship, which was so crowded that each had scarcely room to turn himself, almost suffocated us. This produced copious perspirations, so that the air soon became unfit for respiration, from a variety of loathsome smells, and brought on a sickness among the slaves, of which many died, thus falling victims to the improvident avarice, as I may call it, of their purchasers.

This wretched situation was again aggravated by the galling of the chains, now become insupportable; and the filth of the necessary tubs, into which the children often fell, and were almost suffocated. The shrieks of the women, and the groans of the dying, rendered the whole a scene of horror almost inconceivable.

Happily perhaps for myself I was soon reduced so low here that it was thought necessary to keep me almost always on deck; and from my extreme youth I was not put in fetters. In this situation I expected every hour to share the fate of my companions, some of whom were almost daily brought upon deck at the point of death, which I began to hope would soon put an end to my miseries. Often did I think many of the inhabitants of the deep much more happy than myself. I envied them the freedom they enjoyed, and as often wished I could change my condition for theirs.

Every circumstance I met with served only to render my state more painful, and heightened my apprehensions, and my opinion of the cruelty of the whites. One day they had taken a number of fishes; and when they had killed and satisfied themselves with as many as they thought fit, to our astonishment who were on the deck, rather than give any of them to us to eat, as we expected, they tossed the remaining fish into the sea again, although we begged and prayed for some as well as we could, but in vain. Some of my countrymen, being pressed by hunger, took an opportunity, when they thought no one saw them, of trying to get a little privately; but they were discovered, and the attempt procured them some very severe floggings.

One day, when we had a smooth sea and moderate wind, two of my wearied countrymen who were chained together (I was near them at the time), preferring death to such a life of misery, somehow made through the nettings and jumped into the sea: immediately another quite dejected fellow, who on account of his illness was suffered to be out of irons, also followed their example; and I believe many more would very soon have done the same if they had not been prevented by the ship's crew who were instantly alarmed.

Those of us that were the most active were in a moment put down under the deck, and there was such a noise and confusion amongst the people of the ship as I never heard before, to stop her, and get the boat out to go after the slaves. However two of the wretches were drowned, but they got the other, and afterwards flogged him unmercifully for thus attempting to prefer death to slavery.

In this manner we continued to undergo more hardships than I can now relate, hardships which are inseparable from this accursed trade. Many a time we were near suffocation from the want of fresh air, which we were often without for whole days together. This, and the stench of the necessary tubs, carried off many.

During our passage I first saw flying fishes, which surprised me very much: they used frequently to fly across the ship, and many of them fell on the deck. I also now first saw the use of the quadrant; I had often with astonishment seen the mariners make observations with it, and I could not think what it meant. They at last took notice of my surprise: and one of them, willing to increase it, as well as to gratify my curiosity, made me one day look through it. The clouds appeared to me to be land, which disappeared as they passed along. This heightened my wonder; and I was now more persuaded than ever that I was in another world, and that every thing about me was magic.

At last we came in sight of the island of Barbadoes, at which the whites on board gave a great shout, and made many signs of joy to us. We did not know what to think of this; but as the vessel drew nearer we plainly saw the harbour, and other ships of different kinds and sizes; and we soon anchored amongst them off Bridge-Town.

Many merchants and planters now came on board, though it was in the evening. They put us in separate parcels, and examined us attentively. They also made us jump, and pointed to the land, signifying we were to go there. We thought by this we should be eaten by these ugly men, as they appeared to us; and, when soon after we were all put down under the deck again, there was much dread and trembling.

From *The Interesting Narrative of the Life of Olaudah Equiano, or Gustavus Vassa the African. Written by Himself,* 1791.

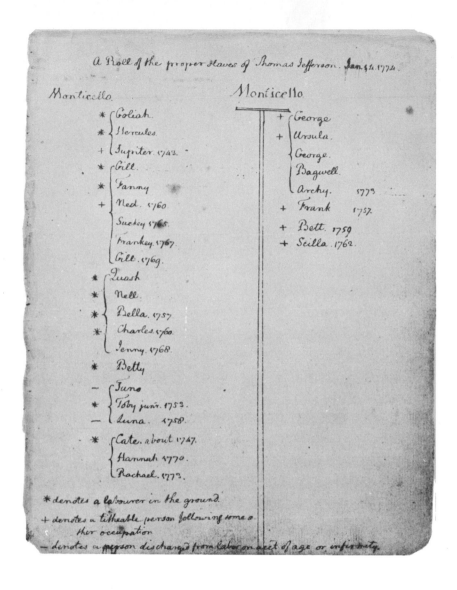

Thomas Jefferson, the third pres-
ident of the United States, was a slaveholder. But he hated
slavery. It degraded both the master and the slave, he believed.
Yet, like many others of his time, he thought Negroes were

inferior to whites in body and mind. In 1792, while Secretary of State in Washington's Cabinet, he received a letter from a free Negro which helped to change his mind.

The writer was Benjamin Banneker, born in 1731 in Maryland. As a young farmer he had shown astonishing mechanical skill when he built a clock out of wooden materials. A Quaker who settled nearby loaned him books on astronomy and some surveying instruments. Fascinated by the world of mathematics, Banneker was soon able to correct errors in the texts and predict a solar eclipse. His genius won him appointment to the commission to plan and survey the new city of Washington. By the 1790's he was editing a series af almanacs which earned him popular favor at home and abroad.

Jefferson, ready to admit error, sent the manuscript copy of the almanac and Banneker's letter to the Academy of Sciences in Paris as a proof of Negro equality.

Banneker to Jefferson . . .

1792

I SUPPOSE IT IS a truth too well attested to you, to need a proof here, that we are a race of beings, who have long labored under the abuse and censure of the world; that we have long been looked upon with an eye of contempt; and that we have long been considered rather as brutish than human, and scarcely capable of mental endowments.

Sir, I hope I may safely admit, in consequence of that report which hath reached me, that you are a man less inflexible in sentiments of this nature, than many others; that you are measurably friendly, and well disposed towards us; and that you are willing and ready to lend your aid and assistance to our relief, from those many distresses, and numerous calamities, to which we are reduced.

Now Sir, if this is founded in truth, I apprehend you will embrace every opportunity to eradicate that train of absurd and false ideas and opinions, which so generally prevails with respect to us; and that your sentiments are concurrent with mine, which are, that one universal Father hath given being to us all; and that he hath not only made us all of one flesh, but that he hath also, without partiality, afforded us all the same sensations and endowed us all with the same faculties; and that however variable we may be in society or religion, however diversified in situation or color, we are all in the same family and stand in the same relation to him . . . .

Sir, I freely and cheerfully acknowledge, that I am of the African race, and in that color which is natural to them of the deepest dye; and it is under a sense of the most profound gratitude to the Supreme Ruler of the Universe, that I now confess to you, that I am not under that state of tyrannical thraldom, and inhuman captivity, to which too many of my brethren are doomed, but that I have abundantly tasted of the fruition of those blessings, which proceed from that free and unequalled liberty with which you are favored . . . .

Sir, suffer me to recall to your mind that time, in which the arms and tyranny of the British crown were exerted, with every powerful effort, in order to reduce you to a state of servitude . . . .

This, Sir, was a time when you clearly saw into the injustice of a state of slavery, and in which you had just apprehensions of the horror of its condition. It was now that your abhorrence thereof was so excited, that you publicly held forth this true and invaluable doctrine, which is worthy to be recorded and remembered in all succeeding ages: "We hold these truths to be self-evident, that all men are created equal; that they are endowed by their Creator with certain unalienable rights, and that among these are, life, liberty, and the pursuit of happiness."

14

Compare slavery to British rule

Here was a time, in which your tender feelings for your-selves had engaged you thus to declare, you were then im-pressed with proper ideas of the great violation of liberty, and the free possession of those blessings, to which you were en-titled by nature; but Sir, how pitiable is it to reflect, that although you were so fully convinced of the benevolence of the Father of Mankind, and of his equal and impartial distribution of these rights and privileges, which he hath conferred upon them, that you should at the same time counteract his mercies, in detaining by fraud and violence so numerous a part of my brethren, under groaning captivity, and cruel oppression, that you should at the same time be found guilty of that most crim-inal act, which you professedly detested in others, with respect to yourselves.

I suppose that your knowledge of the situation of my breth-ren is too extensive to need a recital here; neither shall I pre-sume to prescribe methods by which they may be relieved, oth-erwise than by recommending to you and all others, to wean yourselves from those narrow prejudices which you have im-bibed with respect to them, and as Job proposed to his friends, "put your soul in their souls' stead"; thus shall your hearts be enlarged with kindness and benevolence towards them; and thus shall you need neither the direction of myself or others, in what manner to proceed herein.

And now, Sir, although my sympathy and affection for my brethren hath caused my enlargement thus far, I ardently hope that your candor and generosity will plead with you in my be-half, when I make known to you, that it was not originally my design; but having taken up my pen in order to direct to you, as a present, a copy of my Almanac, which I have calculated for the succeeding year, I was unexpectedly and unavoidably led thereto.

This calculation is the product of my arduous study, in this most advanced stage of life; for having long had unbounded desires to become acquainted with the secrets of nature, I have had to gratify my curiosity herein through my own assiduous application to Astronomical Study, in which I need not recount to you the many difficulties and disadvantages which I have had to encounter.

From *Letter from Benjamin Banneker to the Secretary of State,* 1792.

FREEDOM'S JOURNAL.

"RIGHTEOUSNESS EXALTETH A NATION."

CORNISH & RUSSWURM,
Editors & Proprietors

NEW-YORK, FRIDAY, MARCH 23, 1827.

[VOL. I. No. 2.

MEMOIRS OF CAPT. PAUL CUFFEE.

At this time, being about twenty years of age, he thought himself sufficiently skilled to enter into business on his own account. He laid before his brother David, a plan for opening a commercial intercourse with the state of Connecticut. His brother was pleased with the prospect, they built an open boat and proceeded to sea. Here for the first time his brother found himself exposed to the perils of the ocean, and the hazard of a predatory warfare which was carried on by the Refugees. [...]

To be Continued.

From the Christian Spectator.

PEOPLE OF COLOUR.

The many recent movements in behalf of the children of Africa, give strong indications that better times are approaching for that portion of the human family. [...]

A FRAGMENT.

In one of those delightful autumnal evenings, in the month of October, when the celestial heavens appear in all their splendor and magnificence, [...]

Antislavery newspapers began in 1821, when the white editor Benjamin Lundy launched his Genius of Universal Emancipation *with six subscribers. It was even harder to start the first Negro newspaper,* Freedom's Journal. *It was founded in New York in March, 1827 by John B. Russwurm and Samuel E. Cornish. Young Russwurm had just graduated from Bowdoin, with the first college degree given a Negro in the United States. When he sailed for Liberia in 1829 to become the new republic's superintendent of education, the Reverend Mr. Cornish carried on as editor.*

In their first editorial, the editors struck at prejudice and slavery.

17

Freedom's Journal . . .

1827

(margin, handwritten) Speak for themselves

WE WISH TO plead our own cause. Too long have others spoken for us. Too long has the publick been deceived by misrepresentations, in things which concern us dearly . . . .

The civil rights of a people being of the greatest value, it shall ever be our duty to vindicate our brethren, when oppressed; to lay the case before the publick. We shall also urge upon our brethren (who are qualified by the laws of the different states), the expediency of using their elective franchise; and of making an independent use of the same. We wish them not to become the tools of party . . . .

It is our earnest wish to make our Journal a medium of intercourse between our brethren in the different states of this great confederacy: that through its columns an expression of our sentiments, on many interesting subjects which concern us, may be offered to the publick: that plans which apparently are beneficial may be candidly discussed and properly weighed;

if worth, receive our cordial approbation; if not, our marked disapprobation.

Useful knowledge of every kind, and everything that relates to Africa, shall find a ready admission into our columns; and as that vast continent becomes daily more known, we trust that many things will come to light, proving that the natives of it are neither so ignorant nor stupid as they have generally been supposed to be . . . .

We would not be unmindful of our brethren who are still in the iron fetters of bondage. They are our kindred by all the ties of nature . . . .

From the press and the pulpit we have suffered much by being incorrectly represented . . . .

Our vices and our degradation are ever arrayed against us, but our virtues are passed by unnoticed. And what is still more lamentable, our friends, to whom we concede all the principles of humanity and religion, from these very causes seem to have fallen into the current of popular feeling and are imperceptibly floating on the stream—actually living in the practice of prejudice, while they abjure it in theory, and feel it not in their hearts. END

Is it not very desirable that such should know more of our actual condition; and of our efforts and feelings, that in forming or advocating plans for our amelioration, they may do it more understandingly? In the spirit of candor and humility we intend by a simple representation of facts to lay our case before the public, with a view to arrest the progress of prejudice, and to shield ourselves against the consequent evils. We wish to conciliate all and to irritate none, yet we must be firm and unwavering in our principles, and persevering in our efforts.

If ignorance, poverty and degradation have hitherto been our unhappy lot; has the Eternal decree gone forth, that our race alone are to remain in this state, while knowledge and civilization are shedding their enlivening rays over the rest of the human family? . . .

The interesting fact that there are five hundred thousand free persons of colour, one half of whom might peruse, and the whole be benefitted by the publication of the Journal; that no publication, as yet, has been devoted exclusively to their improvement—that many selections from approved standard authors, which are within the reach of few, may occasionally be made—and more important still, that this large body of our citizens have no public channel—all serve to prove the real necessity, at present, for the appearance of the *Freedom's Journal.*

From *Freedom's Journal,* March 16, 1827.

It is a pity," a Southern planter wrote his brother in 1802, "that agreeable to the nature of things Slavery and Tyranny must go together and that there is no such thing as having an obedient and useful slave, without the painful exercise of undue and tyrannical authority."

Masters knew that Negroes were not natural-born slaves, though they did not scruple to say the opposite. Fear of slave rebellions and knowledge that the law was on the master's side made white men often act brutally. Only three months after Freedom's Journal was founded, a Negro slave was lynched by a mob in Tuscaloosa, Alabama. The news travelled north slowly, finding its way into the Negro newspaper on August 3, 1827.

A lynching report . . .
1827

HORRID OCCURRENCE.—Some time during the last week one of those outrageous transactions—and we really think, disgraceful to the character of civilized man, took place near the north east boundary line of Perry, adjoining Bibb and Autanga counties.

The circumstances, we are informed by a gentleman from that county, are— That a Mr. McNeily having lost some clothing or some other property, of no great value, the slave of a neighboring planter was charged with the theft. McNeily, in company with his brother, found the Negro driving his master's wagon, they seized him, and either did or were about to chastise him, when the Negro stabbed McNeily, so that he died in an hour afterwards.

The Negro was taken before a Justice of the Peace, who, after serious deliberation, waived his authority—perhaps through fear, as the crowd of persons from the above counties had collected to the number of seventy or eighty, near Mr.

People's (the justice) house. He acted as President of the mob, and put the vote, when it was decided he should be immediately executed by being burnt to death—then the sable culprit was led to a tree and tied to it, and a large quantity of pine knots collected and placed around him, and the fatal torch was applied to the pile, even against the remonstrances of several gentlemen who were present; and the miserable being was in a short time consumed to ashes.

An inquest was held over the remains and the Sheriff of Perry county, with a company of about twenty men, repaired to the neighborhood where this barbarous act took place, to secure those concerned, but with what success we have not heard, but we hope he will succeed in bringing the perpetrators of so high-handed a measure to account to their country for their conduct in this affair. This is the second Negro who has been thus put to death, without Judge or Jury in that county.

From *Freedom's Journal,* August 3, 1827.

D avid Walker didn't have to be told that if a slave struck his master it meant death. Free-born in North Carolina, but the son of a slave father, he knew slavery—what the South called the "peculiar institution"—firsthand. His hatred of slavery drove him to Boston, where he sold old clothes and subscriptions to Freedom's Journal. He burned to deliver his own message to the slaves, and in 1829 published his pamphlet, Walker's Appeal. It was a harsh outcry against the injustices done the Negro, and an open call to rise up in arms and overthrow slavery. In a year it ran through three editions, terrifying the slaveholders. Georgia offered $10,000 for Walker taken alive and $1,000 for him dead. State after state in the South made it a crime to circulate the Appeal, and a crime to teach Negroes to read. Suddenly, Walker disappeared; some said, murdered. But the Appeal went on, slashing like a sword at ignorance and docility.

Walker's Appeal . . .

1829

MY BELOVED BRETHREN: The In-
dians of North and of South America—the Greeks—the Irish,
subjected under the king of Great Britain—the Jews, that an-
cient people of the Lord—the inhabitants of the islands of the
sea—in fine, all the inhabitants of the earth (except however,
the sons of Africa), are called *men,* and of course are, and
ought to be free. But we (coloured people), and our children
are *brutes!!* and of course are, and *ought to be* SLAVES to the
American people and their children forever!! to dig their mines
and work their farms; and thus go on enriching them, from one
generation to another with our *blood* and our *tears!!!!* . . . .
They think because they hold us in their infernal chains of
slavery, that we wish to be white, or of their color—but they
are dreadfully deceived—we wish to be just as it pleased our
Creator to have made us, and no avaricious and unmerciful
wretches have any business to make slaves of, or hold us in
slavery. How would they like for us to make slaves of, and hold

them in cruel slavery, and murder them as they do us? . . .

Fear not the number and education of our *enemies,* against whom we shall have to contend for our lawful right; guaranteed to us by our Makers; for why should we be afraid, when God is, and will continue (if we continue humble), to be on our side?

The man who would not fight under our Lord and Master Jesus Christ, in the glorious and heavenly cause of freedom and of God—to be delivered from the most wretched, abject and servile slavery, that ever a people was afflicted with since the foundation of the world, to the present day—ought to be kept with all of his children or family, in slavery, or in chains, to be butchered by his *cruel enemies* . . . .

If you commence, make sure work—do not trifle, for they will not trifle with you—they want us for their slaves, and think nothing of murdering us in order to subject us to that wretched condition—therefore, if there is an *attempt* made by us, kill or be killed. Now, I ask you, had you not rather be killed than to be a slave to a tyrant, who takes the life of your mother, wife, and dear little children? Look upon your mother, wife, and children, and answer God Almighty; and believe this, that it is no more harm for you to kill a man, who is trying to kill you, than it is for you to take a drink of water when thirsty; in fact, the man who will stand still and let another murder him, is worse than an infidel, and, if he has common sense, ought not to be pitied . . . .

Remember Americans, that we must and shall be free and enlightened as you are, will you wait until we shall, under God, obtain our liberty by the crushing arm of power? Will it not be dreadful for you? I speak Americans for your good. We must and shall be free I say, in spite of you. You may do your best to keep us in wretchedness and misery, to enrich you and your children, but God will deliver us from under you. And wo, wo, will be to you if we have to obtain our freedom by fighting. Throw away your fears and prejudices then, and enlighten us and treat us like men, and we will like you more than we do now hate you, and tell us no more about colonization, for America is as much our country, as it is yours.

Treat us like men, and there is no danger but we will all live in peace and happiness together. For we are not like you, hard hearted, unmerciful, and unforgiving. What a happy country this will be, if the whites will listen. What nation under heaven will be able to do any thing with us, unless God gives us up into its hand?

But Americans, I declare to you, while you keep us and our children in bondage, and treat us like brutes, to make us support you and your families, we cannot be your friends. You do not look for it, do you? Treat us then like men, and we will be your friends. And there is not a doubt in my mind, but that the whole of the past will be sunk into oblivion, and we yet, under God, will become a united and happy people. The whites may say it is impossible, but remember that nothing is impossible with God.

From *Walker's Appeal, in Four Articles: Together with a Preamble, to the Colored Citizens of the World, but in particular, and very expressly, to those of the United States of America, written in Boston, State of Massachusetts, September 28, 1829.*

A year after David Walker vanished, the Virginia slave Nat Turner, as if in response to Walker's Appeal, led seventy Negroes in a revolt that slaughtered fifty-seven men, women, and children in rural Southampton County. Troops rushed in to put down the uprising and killed over one hundred Negroes—the innocent as well as the insurrectionists—in a savage massacre. Wild rumors and alarms swept through the South. The apparition of slave revolt made sleep uneasy.

But it was not the first time. Rebellions began in the seventeenth century, aboard the first slave ships bound for the American colonies. As slaves continued to fight for their freedom, the bondage laws were made harsher and harsher. Gabriel Prosser's large-scale plot to attack Richmond with a thousand *men in 1800 was betrayed at the last moment and the slave preacher and his followers hanged. Another plot, led by the free Negro Denmark Vesey, was exposed in Charleston in 1822 and Vesey and thirty-six others executed.*

Nat Turner was educated and a preacher. He believed God had chosen him to deliver his people from bondage. As he lay in prison, waiting to go to the gallows, he made this statement about his life and his mission.

Nat Turner's revolt . . .

1831

I WAS THIRTY-ONE YEARS OF AGE the second of October last, and born the property of Benjamin Turner, of this county. In my childhood a circumstance occurred which made an indelible impression on my mind, and laid the groundwork of that enthusiasm which has terminated so fatally to many, both white and black, and for which I am about to atone at the gallows. It is here necessary to relate this circumstance. Trifling as it may seem, it was the commencement of that belief which has grown with time; and even now, sir, in this dungeon, helpless and forsaken as I am, I cannot divest myself of.

Being at play with other children, when three or four years old, I was telling them something, which my mother, overhearing, said it had happened before I was born. I stuck to my story, however, and related some things which went, in her opinion, to confirm it. Others being called on, were greatly astonished, knowing that these things had happened, and caused them to say, in my hearing, I surely would be a prophet, as the Lord had shown me things that had happened before my birth. And my mother and grandmother strengthened me in this my first impression, saying, in my presence, I was intended for some great purpose, which they had always thought from certain marks on my head and breast . . . .

On the 12th of May, 1828, I heard a loud noise in the heavens, and the Spirit instantly appeared to me and said the Serpent was loosened, and Christ had laid down the yoke he had borne for the sins of men, and that I should take it on and fight against the Serpent, for the time was fast approaching when the first should be last and the last should be first.

Question: "Do you not find yourself mistaken now?"

Answer: "Was not Christ crucified?"

And by signs in the heavens that it would make known to me when I should commence the great work, and until the first sign appeared I should conceal it from the knowledge of men; and on the appearance of the sign (the eclipse of the sun, last February), I should arise and prepare myself, and slay my enemies with their own weapons.

And immediately on the sign appearing in the heavens, the seal was removed from my lips, and I communicated the great work laid out for me to do, to four in whom I had the greatest confidence (Henry, Hark, Nelson, and Sam). It was intended by us to have begun the work of death on the 4th of July last. Many were the plans formed and rejected by us, and it affected my mind to such a degree that I fell sick, and the time passed without our coming to any determination how to commence— still forming new schemes and rejecting them, when the sign appeared again, which determined me not to wait longer.

Since the commencement of 1830 I had been living with Mr. Joseph Travis, who was to me a kind master, and placed the greatest confidence in me; in fact, I had no cause to complain of his treatment to me. On Saturday evening, the 20th of August, it was agreed between Henry, Hark, and myself, to prepare a dinner the next day for the men we expected, and then to concert a plan, as we had not yet determined on any. Hark, on the following morning, brought a pig, and Henry brandy; and being joined by Sam, Nelson, Will, and Jack, they prepared in the woods a dinner, where, about three o'clock I joined them . . . .

I saluted them on coming up, and asked Will how came he there. He answered, his life was worth no more than others, and his liberty as dear to him. I asked him if he thought to obtain it. He said he would, or lose his life. This was enough to put him in full confidence. Jack, I knew, was only a tool in the hands of Hark. It was quickly agreed we should commence at home (Mr. J. Travis') on that night; and until we had armed and equipped ourselves, and gathered sufficient force, neither age nor sex was to be spared—which was invariably adhered to. We remained at the feast until about two hours in the night, when we went to the house and found Austin . . . .

I took my station in the rear, and, as it was my object to carry terror and devastation wherever we went, I placed fifteen or twenty of the best armed and most to be relied on in front, who generally approached the houses as fast as their horses could run. This was for two purposes—to prevent their escape, and strike terror to the inhabitants; on this account I never got to the houses, after leaving Mrs. Whitehead's, until the murders were committed, except in one case. I sometimes got in sight in time to see the work of death completed; viewed the mangled bodies as they lay, in silent satisfaction, and immediately started in quest of other victims.

Having murdered Mrs. Waller and ten children, we started for Mr. Wm. Williams'—having killed him and two little boys that were there; while engaged in this, Mrs. Williams fled and got some distance from the house, but she was pursued, overtaken, and compelled to get up behind one of the company, who brought her back, and after showing her the mangled body of her lifeless husband, she was told to get down and lay by his side, where she was shot dead.

The white men pursued and fired on us several times. Hark had his horse shot under him, and I caught another for him as it was running by me; five or six of my men were wounded, but none left on the field. Finding myself defeated here, I instantly determined to go through a private way, and cross the Nottoway River at the Cypress Bridge, three miles below Jerusalem, and attack that place in the rear, as I expected they would look for me on the other road, and I had a great desire to get there to procure arms and ammunition. After going a short distance in this private way, accompanied by about twenty men, I overtook two or three, who told me the others were dispersed in every direction.

On this, I gave up all hope for the present; and on Thursday night, after having supplied myself with provisions from Mr. Travis', I scratched a hole under a pile of fence-rails in a field, where I concealed myself for six weeks, never leaving my hiding-place but for a few minutes in the dead of the night to get water, which was very near. Thinking by this time I could venture out, I began to go about in the night, and eavesdrop the houses in the neighborhood; pursuing this course for about a fortnight, and gathering little or no intelligence, afraid of speaking to any human being, and returning every morning to my cave before the dawn of the day.

I know not how long I might have led this life, if accident had not betrayed me. A dog in the neighborhood passing by my hiding-place one night while I was out, was attracted by some meat I had in my cave, and crawled in and stole it, and was coming out just as I returned. A few nights after, two Negroes having started to go hunting with the same dog, and passed that way, the dog came again to the place, and having just gone out to walk about, discovered me and barked; on which, thinking myself discovered, I spoke to them to beg concealment. On making myself known, they fled from me. Knowing then they would betray me, I immediately left my hiding-place, and was pursued almost incessantly, until I was taken, a fortnight afterwards, by Mr. Benjamin Phipps, in a little hole I had dug out with my sword, for the purpose of concealment, under the top of a fallen tree.

During the time I was pursued, I had many hair-breadth escapes, which your time will not permit you to relate. I am here loaded with chains, and willing to suffer the fate that awaits me.

From *The Confessions of Nat Turner, the leader of the late insurrection in Southampton, Va.*, edited by Thomas R. Gray, 1831.

T he purpose of slavery was to provide the labor which could bring profits to the master. Most Southern farmers had small holdings and few or no slaves. The wealthy slaveholders, who ruled the South's economy and politics, owned huge plantations with hundreds and thousands of slaves. Whether the estate was large or small, an efficient owner made money out of his slaves. Down to the Civil War it was more profitable for the planter to keep his workers in bondage than to use free labor.

Defenders of slavery claimed the bondsmen cheerfully accepted their condition. But how did the slave look at the year-round routine of growing cotton? One record of what it was like in Louisiana was left by the ex-slave, Solomon Northup. Northup, born free, was kidnapped in Washington and enslaved for twelve years in Louisiana. His story, taken down by a Northerner in the year of his rescue, 1853, sold twenty-seven thousand copies in two years.

Picking cotton ...

1845

THE GROUND IS prepared by throwing up beds or ridges, with the plough—back-furrowing, it is called. Oxen and mules, the latter almost exclusively, are used in ploughing. The women as frequently as the men perform this labor, feeding, currying, and taking care of their teams, and in all respects doing the field and stable work, precisely as do the ploughboys of the North.

The beds, or ridges, are six feet wide, that is, from water furrow to water furrow. A plough drawn by one mule is then run along the top of the ridge or center of the bed, making the drill, into which a girl usually drops the seed, which she carries in a bag hung round her neck. Behind her comes a mule and harrow, covering up the seed, so that two mules, three slaves, a plough and harrow, are employed in planting a row of cotton.

This is done in the months of March and April. Corn is planted in February. When there are no cold rains, the cotton usually makes its appearance in a week. In the course of eight or ten days afterwards the first hoeing is commenced. This is performed in part, also, by the aid of the plough and mule. The plough passes as near as possible to the cotton on both sides, throwing the furrow from it. Slaves follow with their hoes, cutting up the grass and cotton, leaving hills two feet and a half apart. This is called scraping cotton.

In two weeks more commences the second hoeing. This time the furrow is thrown towards the cotton. Only one stalk, the largest, is now left standing in each hill. In another fortnight it is hoed the third time, throwing the furrow towards the cotton in the same manner as before, and killing all the grass between the rows.

About the first of July, when it is a foot high or thereabouts, it is hoed the fourth and last time. Now the whole space between the rows is ploughed, leaving a deep water furrow in the center. During all these hoeings the overseer or driver follows the slaves on horseback with a whip, such as has been described. The fastest hoer takes the lead row. He is usually about a rod in advance of his companions. If one of them passes him, he is whipped. If one falls behind or is a moment idle, he is whipped. In fact, the lash is flying from morning until night, the whole day long. The hoeing season thus continues from April until July, a field having no sooner been finished once, than it is commenced again.

In the latter part of August begins the cotton picking season. At this time each slave is presented with a sack. A strap is fastened to it, which goes over the neck, holding the mouth of the sack breast high, while the bottom reaches nearly to the ground. Each one is also presented with a large basket that will hold about two barrels. This is to put the cotton in when the sack is filled. The baskets are carried to the field and placed at the beginning of the rows.

When a new hand, one unaccustomed to the business, is sent for the first time into the field, he is whipped up smartly, and made for that day to pick as fast as he can possibly. At night it is weighed, so that his capability in cotton picking is known. He must bring in the same weight each night following. If it falls short, it is considered evidence that he has been laggard, and a greater or less number of lashes is the penalty.

An ordinary day's work is two hundred pounds. A slave who is accustomed to picking is punished if he or she brings in a less quantity than that. There is a great difference among them as regards this kind of labor. Some of them seem to have a natural knack, or quickness, which enables them to pick with great celerity, and with both hands, while others, with whatever practice or industry, are utterly unable to come up to the ordinary standard. Such hands are taken from the cotton field and employed in other business . . . .

The hands are required to be in the cotton field as soon as it is light in the morning, and, with the exception of ten or fifteen minutes, which is given them at noon to swallow their allowance of cold bacon, they are not permitted to be a moment idle until it is too dark to see and when the moon is full they often times labor till the middle of the night. They do not dare to stop even at dinner time, nor return to the quarters, however late it be, until the order to halt is given by the driver.

The day's work over in the field, the baskets are "toted," or in other words, carried to the gin-house, where the cotton is weighed. No matter how fatigued and weary he may be—no matter how much he longs for sleep and rest—a slave never approaches the gin-house with his basket of cotton but with fear. If it falls short in weight—if he has not performed the full task appointed him, he knows that he must suffer. And if he has exceeded it by ten or twenty pounds, in all probability his master will measure the next day's task accordingly.

So, whether he has too little or too much, his approach to the gin-house is always with fear and trembling. Most frequently they have too little, and therefore it is they are not anxious to leave the field. After weighing, follow the whippings; and then the baskets are carried to the cotton house, and their contents stored away like hay, all hands being sent in to tramp it down. If the cotton is not dry, instead of taking it to the gin-house at once, it is laid upon platforms, two feet high, and some three times as wide, covered with boards or plank, with narrow walks running between them.

This done, the labor of the day is not yet ended, by any means. Each one must then attend to his respective chores. One feeds the mules, another the swine—another cuts the wood, and so forth; besides, the packing is all done by candle light. Finally, at a late hour, they reach the quarters, sleepy and overcome with the long day's toil. Then a fire must be kindled in the cabin, the corn ground in a small hand-mill, and supper, and dinner for the next day in the field, prepared. All that is allowed them is corn and bacon, which is given out at the corncrib and smoke-house every Sunday morning. Each one receives, as his weekly allowance, three and a half pounds of bacon, and corn enough to make a peck of meal. That is all —no tea, coffee, sugar, and with the exception of a very scanty sprinkling now and then, no salt . . . .

The softest couches in the world are not to be found in the log mansion of the slave. The one whereon I reclined, year after year, was a plank twelve inches wide and ten feet long. My pillow was a stick of wood. The bedding was a coarse blanket, and not a rag or shred beside. Moss might be used, were it not that it directly breeds a swarm of fleas.

The cabin is constructed of logs, without floor or window. The latter is altogether unnecessary, the crevices between the logs admitting sufficient light. In stormy weather the rain drives through them, rendering it comfortless and extremely disagreeable. The rude door hangs on great wooden hinges. In one end is constructed an awkward fire-place.

An hour before day light the horn is blown. Then the slaves arouse, prepare their breakfast, fill a gourd with water, in another deposit their dinner of cold bacon and corn cake, and hurry to the field again. It is an offence invariably followed by a flogging, to be found at the quarters after daybreak. Then the fears and labors of another day begin; and until its close there is no such thing as rest. He fears he will be caught lagging through the day; he fears to approach the gin-house with his basket-load of cotton at night; he fears, when he lies down, that he will oversleep himself in the morning. Such is a true, faithful, unexaggerated picture and description of the slave's daily life, during the time of cotton-picking, on the shores of Bayou Boeuf.

From *Twelve Years a Slave,* by Solomon Northup, 1853.

I*n the middle 1930's fieldwork-*
ers of the Federal Writers' Project were assigned to travel
through the Southern states to gather the life histories of ex-
slaves. Most of the former slaves were now seventy-five to over
one hundred years old. A set of simple instructions and ques-
tions helped get them to recall and talk freely about the time
of slavery. Dozens of subjects were covered by the questions.
The recollections and father-to-son traditions jotted down by
the interviewers proved a folk history of slavery—"history
from the bottom up"—that adds evidence to such slave nar-
ratives as Northup's, recorded during the abolitionist period.

In what follows you hear the voices of the ex-slaves of one
state, Virginia, as they talk about several aspects of their lives
in slavery.

41

Slavery days . . .

MY MA WAS COOK, an' I used to clean house. I liked dustin' part best 'cause I could git my hands on de books and pictures dat ole Marse had spread out all over his readin' room. Ole Missus used to watch me mos' times to see dat I didn't open no books. Sometimes she would close up all de books an' put 'em on de shelf so's I couldn't see 'em, but Marse never liked her messin' wid his things. Dere was one book dat I was crazy about . . . didn't know nothin' of what it was 'bout, but it had a lot of pictures, Injuns and Kings and Queens wid reefs on dey heads. Used to fly to dat book and hold it lookin' at de pictures whilst I dusted wid de other hand.

One day while in de readin' room I heard a step comin' fum de kitchen. 'Fore I could move, de door open an' someone came in. Thought sure it was Missus, but it was Marsa. He looked at me an' saw what I was doin', but he never said nothin'. I closed de book up an' put it back in place. Was scared fo' many a day dat I was gonna git a hidin', but guess he never tole Missus after all.

HIRED OUT

I recollect how Miss Sarah Anne hired out a bunch of her slaves to de railroad dat dey was buildin' thew de woods. Dey hires slaves in one place an' use dem to cut down de timber and saw it up into ties. Den dey hire hundreds of 'em in de next place. Well, when de railroad come to Pamplin, dey hired all de slaves, an' Miss Sarah Anne's too. An' chile, you orter hear dem slaves singin' when dey go to work in de mornin'. Dey all start a-comin' from all d'rections wid dey ax on dey shoulder, an' de mist an' fog be hangin' over de pines, an' de sun jus' breakin' 'cross de fields. Den de slaves start to sing:

> *A col' frosty mo'nin'*
> *De niggers feelin' good*
> *Take yo' ax upon you' shoulder*
> *Nigger, talk to de wood.*

An' de woods jus' a-ringin' wid dis song. Hundreds of dem jus' a singin' to beat de ban'. Dey be paired up to a tree, an' dey mark de blows by de song. Fus' one chop, den his partner, an' when dey sing TALK dey all chop togedder; an' purty soon dey git de tree ready for to fall an' dey yell "Hi" an' de slaves all scramble out de way quick 'cause you can't tell what way a pine tree gonna fall. An' sometime dey sing it like dis:

> *Dis time tomorrer night*
> *Where will I be?*
> *I'll be gone, gone, gone*
> *Down to Tennessee*

43

De slaves sing dis sorrowful, 'cause some of 'em know dey gonna be beat or whipped, or sol' away. 'Course Miss Sarah Anne ain't sol' none, but ole man Derby what had hundreds wud sell some of his'n ev'y time ole slave trader come 'round. No matter what a slave's hire bring, ole slave trader could beat de price.

FOOD AND CLOTHING

Now you see, dar was good marsas an' bad marsas. Marsas what was good saw dat slaves lived decent an' got plenty to eat. Marsas what was mean an' skinflinty throw em' scraps like dey feed a dog an' don' care what kind of shack dey live in. Warn't no law sayin' dey got to treat slaves decent . . . .

Hoe-cakes was made of meal. You mix a cup of meal wid water an' pat it into small cakes. Grease it if you got grease— dat keep it from stickin'. Den you rake out de ashes an' stick it on de hoe into de bottom of de fire an' cover it up. Let it cook 'bout five minutes, den take it out, rub de ashes off an' pick out de splinters. Wash it off wid warm water an' eat it fo' it cools. Don't taste like nothin' if you let it get cold . . . .

De women folks would spin de cotton, card it and weave it. Den dey could cut it an' sew it. Had to turn everything dey made over to marsa—warn't 'lowed to take nothin' fo' yo'self. Couldn't spin nuf clothes for ev'body. All dat didn't git home-spun got guano bags.

IN SICKNESS AND DEATH

Anytime a slave got sick or had de misery, ole Marsa Tom would give him a dram of whiskey. Sometimes I'd go to Marsa

Tom an' say, "Marsa, I done got a terr'ble cole f'om some-place. Don't spec I gonna be able to work today." Marsa laugh an' say, "Come on, you black rascal. Nothin' wrong wid you. All you want is a drink of whiskey." Den he give it to me. An' sometime I go back to him de second or third time, an' tell him de same thing. Sometime he remember he already give it to me an' sometime he don't. All depend on how much Marsa Tom done took hisself . . . .

Mother always said you got to feed sickness 'cause it's in de blood. Said dat rubbin' was bad, 'cause it jus' rub de pain inside. Mother had a tea fo' ev'y which complaint, even one she used to give fo' child birth . . . .

Dr. Dick taught papa all dey was to be knowed 'bout de medicine business. Was one slave woman dat even Dr. Dick gave up fo' daid. Papa give her some special roots. I ain't gonna tell you what. An' de nex' day de woman could swaller and eat. Papa taught me all de roots. Dere's de master weed, an' de Peter's roots, and May Apple, an' Sweet William, an' plenty mo'. You got to know how to fix 'em, dough . . . .

Now on our place when a slave die, ole overseer would go to de saw mill an' git a twelve inch board, shape it wid a point head and foot, an' dig a grave to fit it. Slaves tie de body to de board dressed in all de puhson's clothes 'cause wouldn't no one ever wear 'em. Whoever wear a dead man's clothes gonna die hisself real soon, dey used to say. John Jasper would go from place to place preachin' funerals fo' slaves. Sometimes dem slaves been daid an' buried a year or mo'. Den one Sunday ole Jasper would preach one big sermon over dem all.

GETTING MARRIED

Didn't have to ask Marsa or nothin.' Just go to Ant Sue an' tell her you want to git mated. She tell us to think 'bout it hard fo' two days, 'cause marryin' was sacred in de eyes of Jesus. Arter two days Mose an' I went back an' say we done thought 'bout it an' still want to git married. Den she called all de slaves arter tasks to pray fo' de union dat God was gonna make. Pray we stay together an' have lots of chillun an' none of 'em git sol' 'way from de parents. Den she lay a broomstick 'cross de sill of de house we gonna live in an' jine our hands together. Fo' we step over it she ast us once mo' if we was sho' we wanted to git married. 'Course we say yes. Den she say, "In de eyes of Jesus step into Holy land of mat-de-money." When we step 'cross de broomstick, we was married. Was bad luck to tech de broomstick. Fo'ks always stepped high 'cause dey didn't want no spell cast on 'em—Ant Sue used to say whichever one teched de stick was gonna die fust . . . .

When you married, you had to jump over a broom three times. Dat was de license. If master seen two slaves together too much he would tell 'em dey was married. Hit didn't make no difference if you wanted to or not; he would put you in de same cabin an' make you live together . . . .

Marsa used to sometimes pick our wives fo' us. If he didn't have on his place enough women for the men, he would wait on de side of de road till a big wagon loaded with slaves come by. Den Marsa would stop de ole nigger-trader and buy you a woman. Wasn't no use tryin' to pick one, cause Marsa wasn't gonna pay but so much for her. All he wanted was a young healthy one who looked like she could have children, whether she was purty or ugly as sin. Den he would lead you an' de woman over to one of de cabins and stan' you on de porch. He wouldn't go in. No Sir. He'd stan' right dere at de do' an' open de Bible to de first thing he come to an' read somepin real fast out of it. Den he close up de Bible an' finish up wid dis verse:

> *Dat you' wife*
> *Dat you' husban'*
> *I'se you' marsa*
> *She you' missus*
> *You married.*

THE FUNNIEST THINGS

Charlie could make up songs 'bout de funnies' things. One day Charlie saw ole Marsa comin' home wid a keg of whiskey on his ole mule. Cuttin' 'cross de plowed field, de ole mule slipped an' Marsa come tumblin' off. Marsa didn't know Charlie saw him, an' Charlie didn't say nothin'. But soon arter a visitor come an' Marsa called Charlie to de house to show off what he knew. Marsa say, "Come here, Charlie, an' sing some rhymes fo' Mr. Henson." "Don't know no new ones, Marsa," Charlie answered. "Come on, you black rascal, give me a rhyme fo' my company—one he ain't heard." So Charlie say, "All right, Marsa, I give you a new one effen you promise not to whup me." Marsa promised, an' den Charlie sung de rhyme he done made up in his haid 'bout Marsa:

> *Jackass rared*
> *Jackass pitch*
> *Throwed ole Marsa in de ditch.*

Well, Marsa got mad as a hornet, but he didn't whup Charlie, not dat time anyway. An' chile, don' you know us used to set de flo' to dat dere song? Mind you, never would sing it when

Marsa was roun', but when he wasn't we'd swing all roun' de cabin singin' 'bout how old Marsa fell off de mule's back. Charlie had a bunch of verses:

> *Jackass stamped*
> *Jackass neighed*
> *Throwed ole Marsa on his haid.*

Don' recoll' all dat smart slave made up. But ev'ybody sho' bus' dey sides laughin' when Charlie sung de las' verse:

> *Jackass stamped*
> *Jackass hupped*
> *Marsa hear you slave, you sho' git whupped.*

RUNAWAYS

I heard a rap—bump! bump! on my do'. I answered a-hollerin! Den someone whispered, "Hush! Don' say nothin', but let me in!" I let her in. Lawd, dat 'oman was all out of bref an' a-beggin'—"Kin I stay here tonight?" I tole her she could, so dar de 'oman done sleep right dar behin' me in my bed all night. I knowed she had runned away, an' I was gonna do my part to he'p her 'long. I took an' heared de hosses an' talkin' in de woods. Dogs jes' a-barkin'. I peeped out de winder an' saw dem white folks go by. I didn't move, I was so scared dey was gonna come in de cabin an' search fo' dat po' 'oman. Nex' mornin' she stole out from dar, an' I ain't never seen her no mo' . . . .

We was workin' on de road one day, an' two fellows named Body an' Ned Coleman slipped off an' ev'y day would sleep in leaves an' hin' trees, an' durin' de night dey would travel. Dey was tryin' to make it to Ohio where you was free. Dey traveled on an' on, night after night. One night dey stopped at a place an' asked for some food an' tol' what dey was doin', an' de people tol' dem dey was 'bout one night's journey from de line. De nex' day dey went to sleep in a wooded place, an' after a while dey heard a noise, an' it was two Newfoundland dogs dat was grazin' de cattle. Dey ran, but de dogs caught dem, an' dey was sent back to de railroad. When dey come back to de railroad de boss beat dem. De boss sent fo' de master to come an' git dem. Dey tole me how near dey was to de line when dem dogs caught dem. Body died soon after. I spec' it was from de whippin'.

PATROLLERS

In dese meetin's ole Jim Bennett, de preacher, didn't know a letter in a book, but he sho' could preach. Dar wasn't no Bible in dem days 'cept what de white folks had, an' dey wan't gwine let no slave see hit even if he could read.

Old Jim would keep a knot of lightwood handy, an' he'd stick hit close to de fire to draw de pitch out it. When de patterollers come to de door 'twas already hot, you see. Preacher would run to de fireplace, git him a light an' take dat torch an' wave hit back an' fo'th so dat de pitch an' fire would be flyin' ev'y which a way in dese patterollers' faces. Out de doors de slaves would go; dar was a mighty scramble an' scuffle in de dark, an' de slaves would scatter in all directions. You see, patterollers was mostly atter de preacher 'cause he was de leader o' de meetin'. Was a terrible lashin' comin' to him dat got caught . . . .

But there was ways of beating the patterollers. De best way was to head 'em off. I 'member once when we was gonna have a meetin' down in de woods near de river. Well, dey made me de lookout boy, an' when de paddyrollers come down de lane past de church—you see dey was 'spectin dat de niggers gonna hold a meetin' dat night—well, sir, dey tell me to step out f'm de woods an' let 'em see me. Well, I does, an' de paddyrollers dat was on horse back come a chasin' arter me, jus' a-gallopin' down de lane to beat de band. Well I was jus' ahead of 'em, an' when they got almost up wid me I jus' ducked into de woods. Course de paddyrollers couldn't stop so quick an' kep' on 'roun' de ben', an' den dere came a-screamin' an' cryin' dat make you think dat hell done bust loose. Dem old paddyrollers done rid plumb into a great line of grape vines dat de slaves had stretched 'cross de path. An' dese vines tripped up de horses an' throwed de ole paddyrollers off in de bushes. An' some done landed mighty hard, cause dey was a-limpin' roun' an' cussin' an' callin' fo' de slaves to come an' help dem, but dem slaves got plenty o' sense. Dey lay in de bushes an' hole dere sides a-laughin', but ain't none o' 'em gonna risk bein' seen. All right dat night, but de nex' mornin' gonna come. Help de white man den but in de mornin' he done forgot all 'bout how you help him. All he know is dat you was out. So after ole paddyrollers go on limpin' back to de town, we go on to de woods an' hold our meetin'.

Arter dat, ole paddyrollers got wise an' used to tie dey horses an' come creepin' thew de woods on foot, tell dey fin' whar dis meetin' was gwine on. Den dey would rush in an' start whippin' an' beatin' de slaves unmerciful. All dis was done to keep you f'om servin' God an' do you know some o' dem devils was mean an' sinful 'nough to say, "If I ketch you here servin' God, I'll beat you. You ain't got no time to serve God. We bought you to serve us."

From *The Negro in Virginia,* sponsored by The Hampton Institute, 1940.

DANIEL A. PAYNE

The first Puritan settlers of New England, believing it their duty to convert their slaves, taught them to read the Bible. Later, the Quakers questioned the right to hold people in slavery and opened schools for slave children. After the Revolution, both private and public schools were established for Negroes in some parts of the North, but in the South the movement was much more cautious. Gabriel's slave revolt in 1800 frightened the planters and from then on schools for Negroes were usually either secret or private.

Laws barred slaves from learning to read. Some Southerners, like Senator John Calhoun, said Negroes could not absorb education. If that were so, why bother with laws to prevent teaching them? Nevertheless, here and there a few slaves would manage to learn, either by themselves, or from *kind masters, or from white playmates. Courageous Negroes and whites dared violate the laws by teaching Negroes in private schools scattered in several Southern states.*

One of these teachers was Daniel A. Payne, a free Negro born in Charleston, South Carolina, in 1811. He became a bishop of the African Methodist Episcopal Church and was elected head of Wilberforce College, the first Negro to be a college president, At eighteen, he opened a private school for Negroes in Charleston, and kept it going for six years, until a state law forced it to close. In his autobiography he tells how he taught himself and others.

Teaching—and learning . . .

1829-1835

MY FIRST SCHOOL was opened in 1829 in a house on Tradd Street occupied by one Caesar Wright. It consisted of his three children, for each of whom he paid me fifty cents a month. I also taught three adult slaves at night, at the same price, thus making my monthly income from teaching only three dollars. This was not sufficient to feed me, but a slave-woman, Mrs. Eleanor Parker, supplied many of my wants. I was happy in my humble employment, but at the end of the year I was so discouraged at the financial result, and by the remarks expressed by envious persons, that I decided to seek some other employment which would yield better pay.

At this juncture a wealthy slave-holder arrived in Charleston, en route to the West Indies for his health. Knowing that British law emancipated every slave that put his foot on British soil, he desired to obtain the services of a free young man of color sufficiently intelligent to do his out-of-door business. I was commended to him, and called upon him at the Planters'

Hotel. Among the inducements he offered he said: "If you will go with me, the knowledge that you will acquire of men and things will be of far more value to you than the wages I will pay you. Do you know what makes the difference between the master and the slave? Nothing but superior knowledge."

This statement was fatal to his desire to obtain my services, for I instantly said to myself: "If it is true that there is nothing but superior knowledge between the master and the slave, I will not go with you, but will rather go and obtain that knowledge which constitutes the master." As I politely took my leave these words passed through my mind:

> *He that flies his Saviour's cross*
> *Shall meet his Maker's frown.*

Then these reflections followed. "In abandoning the school-room am I not fleeing from the cross which the Saviour has imposed upon me? Is not the abandonment of the teacher's work in my case a sin?" The answer was easily found, and I resolved to reopen my school and to inform my patrons to that effect.

On the first of the year 1830 I reopened my school, which continued to increase in numbers until the room became too small, and I was constrained to procure a more commodious place. This in turn became too small, and one was built for me on Anson Street, by Mr. Robert Howard, in the rear of his yard . . . . Here I continued to teach until April, 1835.

During the three years of my attendance at the school of Mr. Thomas S. Bonneau I learned how to read, write, and spell; also arithmetic as far as the "Rule of Three." Spelling was a delightful exercise of my boyhood. In this I excelled.

Seldom did I lose my place at the head of my class, and he who won it did not occupy it long. History was my great delight. Of geography and map-drawing, English grammar and composition, I knew nothing, because they were not taught in any of the schools for colored children. I therefore felt the need of knowledge in these directions; but how was I to obtain it?

I had a geography, but had never seen an atlas, and what was more, I knew not how or where to get one. Fortunately for me, one day as I was sitting on the piazza endeavoring to learn some lesson, a woman entered the gate and approached me with a book in her hand. Said she: "Don't you want to buy this book?" Taking it, I opened it, and to my great joy I beheld the colored maps of an atlas—the very thing I needed. Said I: "What will you take for it?" The woman had found it on the street, and replied: "Whatever you choose to give." All that I could command at the time was a York shilling (twelve and one-half cents in silver coin), so I gave it to her, and rejoiced over my prize.

Immediately I went to work with my geography and atlas, and in about six months was able to construct maps on the Mercator's and globular projection. After I had acquired this ability I introduced geography and map-drawing into my school. At the same time with geography I studied and mastered English grammar. I began with *Murray's Primary Grammar,* and committed the entire book to memory, but did not understand it; so I reviewed it. Then light sprung up; still I felt like one in a dungeon who beheld a glimmer of light at a distance, and with steady but cautious footsteps moved toward it; inspired by the hope that I would soon find its source and come out into the full blaze of animated day. I then made a second review of it, and felt conscious of my power to teach it. I therefore added that to my curriculum.

Having now the groundwork, I began to build the super-structure. I commenced with *Playfair's Euclid,* and proceeded as far as the first five books. The next thing which arrested my attention was botany. The author and her specimens enchanted me; my progress was rapid, and the study became to me a source of great happiness and an instrument of great usefulness. Descriptive chemistry, natural philosophy, and descriptive astronomy followed in rapid succession.

Burret's Geography of the Heavens was my text-book in the last-named science. Stimulated by this interesting guide, I watched the total eclipse of 1832 from its commencement to its completion with my naked eye; but I paid dear for my rash experiment. The immediate result was a partial loss of sight. No book could be read for about three weeks. Whenever I opened a book the pages had the appearance of black sheets. From this injury I have never fully recovered. Up to that time my eyes were like those of the eagle; ever since they have been growing weaker and weaker.

Then, on a Thursday morning, I bought a Greek grammar, a lexicon, and a Greek Testament. On the same day I mastered the Greek alphabet; on Friday I learned to write them; on Saturday morning I translated the first chapter of Matthew's Gospel from Greek into English. My very soul rejoiced and exulted in this glorious triumph. Next came the Latin and the French. Meanwhile I was pushing my studies in drawing and coloring till I was able to produce a respectable flower, fruit, or animal on paper and on velvet.

My researches in botany gave me a relish for zoology; but

as I could never get hold of any work on this science I had to make books for myself. This I did by killing such insects, toads, snakes, young alligators, fishes, and young sharks as I could catch. I then cleaned and stuffed those that I could, and hung them upon the walls of my school-room.

The following fact will give the index of my methods. I bought a live alligator, made one of my pupils provoke him to bite, and whenever he opened his mouth I discharged a load of shot from a small pistol down his throat. As soon as he was stunned I threw him on his back, cut his throat, ripped open his chest, hung him up and studied his viscera till they ceased to move. The flesh of all that I killed I cooked and tasted. I excepted nothing but the toad and snake. My detestations for these was too intense to allow me to put their flesh into my mouth.

My enthusiasm was the inspiration of my pupils. I used to take my first class of boys into the woods every Saturday in search of insects, reptiles, and plants, and at the end of five years I had accumulated some fine specimens of each of these. I had also taken a fatherless boy to educate gratuitously . . . .

In the prosecution of my studies in zoology I desired to obtain a highland moccasin, which was then considered a species of rattlesnake, and whose bite was deadly. Therefore I engaged the services of a slave of lawyer Lionel Kennedy, who was at that time an alderman of the city of Charleston. The plantation of this gentleman was about one mile distant from the city. On the appointed Saturday I dispatched three of my advanced class (John Lee, Robert Wishan, and Michael Eggart) with a large glass bottle, in order that they might bring me the viper alive. On their arrival at the plantation they found Lawyer Kennedy and his son, Dr. Kennedy, overlooking the work of the slaves. They knew me and knew the boys' parents. Calling the lads to them, they demanded the reason of their appearance on the plantation. A direct answer was given. Then they asked the lads to tell them what were the different things taught them, and they also examined them in their studies. The boys answered every question put to them except one. Then said the young doctor: "Why, pa, Payne is playing hell in Charleston." This occurred about the middle of the summer of 1834.

From *Recollections of Seventy Years,*
by Daniel A. Payne, 1888.

O*ne of the most brilliant Amer-icans of the nineteenth century started life as a slave on a Maryland plantation. Frederick Douglass never knew his father and saw his mother only a few times before her death. Until he was eight he lived a hungry, cold, and ragged life. Then he was sent to Baltimore to work first as a servant and later as a shipyard laborer. Slaves were forbidden education, but the boy managed to learn to read and write. And with knowledge came the power to win freedom and a great place in his country's history. In 1838, at the age of twenty-one, he fled slavery. In the years ahead, his growth was spectacular. As lecturer, editor, writer, organizer, diplomat, he earned the leadership of the Negro people in their struggle to emancipate themselves. The story of how Douglass learned his ABC's is part of his book,* Narrative of the Life of Frederick Douglass, *published in 1845. It was a superb autobiography, and immediately popular here and in Europe.*

The ABC's . . .

1845

VERY SOON AFTER I went to live with Mr. and Mrs. Auld, she very kindly commenced to teach me the A, B, C. After I had learned this, she assisted me in learning to spell words of three or four letters. Just at this point of my progress, Mr. Auld found out what was going on, and at once forbade Mrs. Auld to instruct me further, telling her, among other things, that it was unlawful, as well as unsafe, to teach a slave to read.

To use his own words, further, he said, "If you give a nigger an inch, he will take an ell. A nigger should know nothing but to obey his master—to do as he is told to do. Learning would spoil the best nigger in the world. Now," said he, "if you teach that nigger how to read, there would be no keeping him. It would forever unfit him to be a slave. He would at once become unmanageable, and of no value to his master. As to himself, it could do him no good, but a great deal of harm. It would make him discontented and unhappy."

These words sank deep into my heart, stirred up sentiments within that lay slumbering, and called into existence an entirely new train of thought. It was a new and special revelation, explaining dark and mysterious things, with which my youthful understanding had struggled, but struggled in vain. I now understood what had been to me a most perplexing difficulty—to wit, the white man's power to enslave the black man. It was a grand achievement, and I prized it highly.

Though conscious of the difficulty of learning without a teacher, I set out with high hope, and a fixed purpose, at whatever cost of trouble, to learn how to read. The very decided manner with which he spoke, and strove to impress his wife with the evil consequences of giving me instruction, served to convince me that he was deeply sensible of the truths he was uttering. It gave me the best assurance that I might rely with the utmost confidence on the results which, he said, would flow from teaching me to read.

What he most dreaded, that I most desired. What he most loved, that I most hated. That which to him was a great evil, to be carefully shunned, was to me a great good, to be diligently sought; and the argument which he so warmly urged, against my learning to read, only served to inspire me with a desire and determination to learn.

In learning to read, I owe almost as much to the bitter opposition of my master, as to the kindly aid of my mistress. I acknowledge the benefit of both . . . .

My mistress was, as I have said, a kind and tender-hearted woman; and in the simplicity of her soul she commenced, when I first went to live with her, to treat me as she supposed one human being ought to treat another . . . . Slavery proved as injurious to her as it did to me . . . . Under its influence, the tender heart became stone, and the lamblike disposition gave way to one of tigerlike fierceness.

The first step in her downward course was in her ceasing to

instruct me. She now commenced to practice her husband's precepts. She finally became even more violent in her opposition than her husband himself. She was not satisfied with simply doing as well as he had commanded; she seemed anxious to do better. Nothing seemed to make her more angry than to see me with a newspaper. She seemed to think that here lay the danger. I have had her rush at me with a face made all up of fury, and snatch from me a newspaper, in a manner that fully revealed her apprehension. She was an apt woman; and a little experience soon demonstrated, to her satisfaction, that education and slavery were incompatible with each other.

From this time I was most narrowly watched. If I was in a separate room any considerable length of time, I was sure to be suspected of having a book, and was at once called to give an account of myself. All this, however, was too late. The first step had been taken. Mistress, in teaching me the alphabet, had given me the inch, and no precaution could prevent me from taking the ell.

The plan which I adopted, and the one by which I was most successful, was that of making friends of all the little white boys whom I met in the street. As many of these as I could, I converted into teachers. With their kindly aid, obtained at different times and in different places, I finally succeeded in learning to read. When I was sent on errands, I always took my book with me, and by doing one part of my errand quickly, I found time to get a lesson before my return. I used also to carry bread with me, enough of which was always in the house, and to which I was always welcome; for I was much better off in this regard than many of the poor white children in our neighborhood. This bread I used to bestow upon the hungry little urchins, who, in return, would give me that more valuable bread of knowledge . . . .

I was now about twelve years old, and the thought of being a slave for life began to bear heavily upon my heart. Just about this time, I got hold of a book entitled *The Columbian Orator.* Every opportunity I got, I used to read this book. Among much of other interesting matter, I found in it a dialogue between a master and his slave. The slave was represented as having run away from his master three times. The dialogue represented the conversation which took place between them, when the slave was retaken the third time.

In this dialogue, the whole argument in behalf of slavery was brought forward by the master, all of which was disposed of by the slave. The slave was made to say some very smart as well as impressive things in reply to his master—things which had the desired though unexpected effect; for the conversation resulted in the voluntary emancipation of the slave on the part of the master . . . .

The idea as to how I might learn to write was suggested to me by being in Durgin and Bailey's shipyard, and frequently seeing the ship carpenters, after hewing, and getting a piece of timber ready for use, write on the timber the name of that part of the ship for which it was intended.

When a piece of timber was intended for the larboard side, it would be marked thus—"L." When a piece was for the starboard side forward, it would be marked thus—"S.F." For larboard aft, it would be marked thus—"L.A." For starboard aft, it would be marked thus—"S.A." I soon learned the names of these letters, and for what they were intended when placed upon a piece of timber in the shipyard. I immediately commenced copying them, and in a short time was able to make the four letters named.

After that, when I met with any boy who I knew could write, I would tell him I could write as well as he. The next word would be, "I don't believe you. Let me see you try it." I would then make the letters which I had been so fortunate as to learn, and ask him to beat that. In this way I got a good many lessons in writing, which it is quite possible I should never have gotten in any other way.

During this time, my copy-book was the board fence, brick wall, and pavement; my pen and ink was a lump of chalk. With these, I learned mainly how to write. I then commenced and continued copying the Italics on *Webster's Spelling Book,* until I could make them all without looking on the book. By this time, my little Master Thomas had gone to school, and learned how to write, and had written over a number of copy-books. These had been brought home, and shown to some of our near neighbors, and then laid aside. My mistress used to go to class meeting at the Wilk Street meeting-house every Monday afternoon, and leave me to take care of the house. When left thus, I used to spend the time in writing in the spaces left in Master Thomas's copy-book, copying what he had written. I continued to do this until I could write a hand very similar to that of Master Thomas.

Thus, after a long, tedious effort for years, I finally succeeded in learning how to write.

From *Narrative of the Life of Frederick Douglass,* 1845.

FREDERICK DOUGLASS

I didn't know I was a slave until I found out I couldn't do the things I wanted." That was how an old ex-slave put it when he was asked how it felt to be in bondage in childhood. Not having anything to say about the use of your own time and labor was probably what made you feel worst. That was lack of freedom. Of course slaveholders commonly claimed their slaves were cheerful and peaceful, content with their condition. And slaves—humble and smiling in front of their master—would be mad to proclaim their wish to be free, knowing the penalties for showing disloyalty.

There are not many records of how the slave really felt. In his autobiography, Frederick Douglass tells how he first came to question slavery, when he was still a child.

Why am I a slave? . . .

1845

WHY AM I A SLAVE? Why are some people slaves, and others masters? Was there ever a time when this was not so? How did the relation commence?

These were the perplexing questions which began now to claim my thoughts, and to exercise the weak powers of my mind, for I was still but a child, and knew less than children of the same age in the free states. As my questions concerning these things were only put to children a little older, and little better informed than myself, I was not rapid in reaching a solid footing. By some means I learned from these inquiries, that "God, up in the sky," made everybody; and that he made white people to be masters and mistresses, and black people to be slaves.

This did not satisfy me, nor lessen my interest in the subject. I was told, too, that God was good, and that He knew what was best for me, and best for everybody. This was less satisfactory than the first statement; because it came, point blank, against all my notions of goodness. It was not good to let old master cut the flesh off Esther, and make her cry so. Besides, how did people know that God made black people to be slaves? Did they go up in the sky and learn it? or, did He come down and tell them so. All was dark here.

It was some relief to my hard notions of the goodness of God, that, although he made white men to be slaveholders, he did not make them to be bad slaveholders, and that, in due time, he would punish the bad slaveholders; that he would, when they died, send them to the bad place, where they would be "burnt up." Nevertheless, I could not reconcile the relation of slavery with my crude notions of goodness.

Then, too, I found that there were puzzling exceptions to this theory of slavery on both sides, and in the middle. I knew of blacks who were not slaves; I knew of whites who were not slaveholders; and I knew of persons who were nearly white, who were slaves. Color, therefore, was a very unsatisfactory basis for slavery.

Once, however, engaged in the inquiry, I was not very long in finding out the true solution of the matter. It was not color, but crime, not God, but man, that afforded the true explanation of the existence of slavery; nor was I long in finding out another important truth, viz: what man can make, man can unmake.

The appalling darkness faded away, and I was master of the subject. There were slaves here, direct from Guinea; and there were many who could say that their fathers and mothers were stolen from Africa—forced from their homes, and compelled to serve as slaves. This, to me, was knowledge; but it was a kind of knowledge which filled me with a burning hatred of slavery, increased my suffering, and left me without the means of breaking away from my bondage. Yet it was knowledge quite worth possessing.

I could not have been more than seven or eight years old, when I began to make this subject my study. It was with me in the woods and fields; along the shore of the river, and wherever my boyish wanderings led me; and although I was, at that time, quite ignorant of the existence of the free states, I distinctly remember being, even then, most strongly impressed with the idea of being a free man some day. This cheering assurance was an inborn dream of my human nature—a constant menace to slavery—and one which all the powers of slavery were unable to silence or extinguish.

From *Narrative of the Life of Frederick Douglass,* 1845.

As the Northern states one by one prohibited slavery, the number of free Negroes grew. Some were born free, some freed themselves by running away, some were given freedom by their masters, some bought their freedom. One tenth of the million Negroes in the United States in 1800 were free. By the Civil War, there were about five hundred thousand free Negroes, half living in the South and half in the North. They knew only marginal freedom. From the time of the American Revolution that margin had shrunk until it was sometimes hard to tell the difference between slave and freeman. It was easy for whites to claim a Negro was a slave; the law gave the Negro poor chance to defend himself. Kidnapping a free Negro and forcing him into slavery was a common practice. New Yorkers organized a Vigilance Committee to resist kidnappers. In July, 1836, David Ruggles, Negro bookseller and abolitionist who headed the committee, described a kidnapping in this letter to the newspapers.

A kidnapping . . .

1836

IT IS TOO BAD to be told, much less to be endured!— On Saturday, 23d instant, about 12 o'clock, Mr. George Jones, a respectable free colored man, was arrested at 21 Broadway, by certain police officers, upon the pretext of his having "committed assault and battery." Mr. Jones, being conscious that no such charge could be sustained against him, refused to go with the officers. His employers, placing high confidence in his integrity, advised him to go and answer to the charge, promising that any assistance should be afforded to satisfy the end of justice. He proceeded with the officers, accompanied with a gentleman who would have stood his bail—he was locked up in Bridewell—his friend was told that "when he was wanted he could be sent for."

Between the hours of 1 and 2 o'clock, Mr. Jones was carried before the Hon. Richard Riker, Recorder of the City of New York. In the absence of his friends, and in the presence of several notorious kidnappers, who preferred and by oath sustained that he was a runaway slave, poor Jones (having no one to utter a word in his behalf, but a boy, in the absence of numerous friends who could have borne testimony to his freedom), was by the Recorder pronounced to be a SLAVE!

In less than three hours after his arrest, he was bound in chains, dragged through the streets, like beast to the shambles! My depressed countrymen, we are all liable; your wives and children are at the mercy of merciless kidnappers. We have no protection in law, because the legislators withhold justice. We must no longer depend on the interposition of Manumission or Anti-Slavery Societies, in the hope of peaceable and just protection; where such outrages are committed, peace and justice cannot dwell. While we are subject to be thus inhumanly practised upon, no man is safe; we must look to our own safety and protection from kidnappers, remembering that "self-defence is the first law of nature."

Let a meeting be called—let every man who has sympathy in his heart to feel when bleeding humanity is thus stabbed afresh, attend the meeting; let a remedy be prescribed to protect us from slavery. Whenever necessity requires, let that remedy be applied. Come what, any thing is better than slavery.

From *The Liberator,* August 6, 1836.

The fear of being taken back into slavery gnawed constantly at the free Negro. But there were other hardships to be endured. Northern and Southern states denied him the right to vote, his testimony in courts was not accepted if whites were concerned, he paid his taxes but could not send his children to public schools, he was shut out of churches or put into separate pews. "Jim Crow"—words taken from the title of a song popularized by a white "black-face" minstrel—became the term for this segregation based on color. But many Negroes did not accept Jim Crow. In 1838, a Negro named Thomas Van Renselaer wrote a white friend of what happened on a steamboat from Boston to Providence.

Jim Crow aboard ship . . .

1838

DEAR BROTHER,—I stepped on board the Steamboat *J. W. Richmond,* in your city, yesterday afternoon, for Providence. I had previously understood that this being an opposition boat, people were treated irrespective of complexion; so, full of hope of a pleasant entertainment, I went to the office and paid $3.50 (fifty cents more than the regular fare), for my passage and a berth, No. 15, which was assigned me in the after cabin, and obtained my ticket.

I walked about until dark, when, feeling chilly, I repaired to the cabin in which my berth was. I had not been there long, before a man came up to me in a very abrupt manner, and said, "Whose servant are you?" I at first gave no answer; he repeated, and I replied, I am my own, Sir. "Well," said he, "you must go on deck." I asked, why so? "Because you ought to know your place." I said, this is my place. Said he, "Go on deck, I tell you." Said, I, I cannot go on deck. Said he with an oath, and running upon deck, "I'll make you." He returned in

73

a moment with the captain, who came trembling, and said, "I want you to go on deck immediately." I asked the reason. "Not a word from you, sir." I asked, what offence have I committed? "Not a word, sir," said he, and laid hold of me with violence, and ordered two men to remove me.

But when I saw him in such a rage, and fearing that he might do himself harm, I retired, and walked the deck till late at night, when I had another talk with the captain. I then told him he had not treated me well, and that an explanation was due from him, but he refused to allow me to go below, or to give me a berth. I then told him I should publish the treatment I had received. He again flew into a passion, and I saw no more of him.

Between 11 and 12 o'clock, one of the waiters invited me to occupy a bed which he had prepared. I accepted it, and was rendered comfortable and feel very grateful to three of the waiters for their sympathy in these trying moments, as well as to some of the passengers. One gentleman in particular, the Rev. Mr. Scudder (Methodist) gave me great consolation by identifying himself with me at the time.

Now dear brother, I have made this communication of facts for the information of the friends of human rights, who, I believe, have patronized this boat from principle, that they may act accordingly hereafter.

From *The Liberator,* November 30, 1838.

PRUDENCE CRANDALL.

The Negro in the North saw education as a means of raising his economic position and tearing down the barriers of discrimination. With schooling, the Negroes would produce their own leaders in the arts, sciences, and professions.

But proposals to educate Negroes almost always roused sharp opposition in the North. And against the prospect of integration—of Negro and white children sitting together in the same classrooms—law, custom, and popular prejudice combined to erect high walls. Almost everywhere in the North, by

75

the 1830's, Negro children—if they were being educated at all —were attending separate schools.

When shut out of white schools, Negroes determinedly moved to start their own schools. But whites often did not accept these, either. In Ohio, for example, several Negro schools were wrecked and their teachers insulted and beaten. In Connecticut, when antislavery leaders sought to establish a manual training college for Negroes, a New Haven town meeting voted seven hundred to four against it, killing the plan.

In that same year, 1831, a young white Quaker schoolmistress, Prudence Crandall, decided to admit one Negro to her popular girls' boarding school in Canterbury, Connecticut. White parents at once withdrew their children. Miss Crandall then decided to open the school exclusively to Negroes. But stores refused to sell her supplies, the local physician refused to treat the students, the school well was filled with manure, the students insulted on the streets, the school building stoned and burned, and Miss Crandall put in prison. At last she gave up and left the state.

The leader of the campaign against the Crandall school was Andrew T. Judson, political figure and the magistrate who put the teacher in jail. From England he received an ironic letter sent by the Reverend Nathaniel Paul, pastor of the first African Baptist Church in Albany, New York. Paul was then abroad on an antislavery lecturing tour.

About Prudence Crandall . . .

1833

SIR—Through the medium of the American newspapers, I have seen your name, and the names of your worthy coadjutors, and have read your noble and praiseworthy deeds, in regard to the establishment of a school in your town, conducted by one Miss Prudence Crandall, for the instruction of young ladies of color! And believing that acts so patriotic, so republican, so Christian-like in their nature, as yours, against the unpardonable attempts of this fanatical woman, should not be confined to one nation or continent, but that the world should know them, and learn and profit thereby; I have thought proper to do all in my power to spread your fame, that your works may be known at least throughout this country. Nor will you marvel at my magnanimity when I inform you that I am, myself, a native of New England, and consequently proud of whatever may emanate from her sons, calculated to exalt them in the eyes of the world.

And as I have been for some months past and still am engaged in travelling and delivering lectures upon the state of slavery as it exists in the United States, and the condition of the free people of color there, it will afford me an excellent opportunity of making this whole affair known; nor shall I fail to improve it. Yes, sir, Britons shall know that there are men in America, and whole towns of them, too, who are not so destitute of true heroism but that they can assail a helpless woman, surround her house by night, break her windows, and drag her to prison, for the treasonable act of teaching females of color to read!!!

Already is the State of Connecticut indebted to me for my gratuitous services since I have been in this country, in her behalf; especially the city of New-Haven, and its worthy Mayor. Their magnanimous conduct in regard to the establishment of a college for colored youth in that place, I have spread from "Dan to Beersheba"; and Dennis Kimberly [Mayor of New Haven] may rest assured that the name of Benedict Arnold does not stand higher in the estimation of the American people than his does in England! It is my intention, sir, to give you an equal elevation.

I shall make no charge for the service I may render you. Nevertheless, if you think I am truly deserving, and ought to have a compensation, whatever you may feel it your duty to give, you will please to hand it over to the Treasurer of the "American Colonization Society," of which, I understand you are a member and an advocate.

REV. NATHANIEL PAUL

From *The Liberator*, November 23, 1833.

Charles Lenox Remond lived in a comfortable home in Salem, the peaceful Massachusetts town where he was born in 1814. His friends described him as "small in stature, of spare make, neat wiry build, genteel appearance, and pleasant voice." They could have said, too, that he was well educated, brilliant—and black. Only that last point set him apart from his countrymen. Like them, he was born free. But since he was born black, too, he was not a fully franchised citizen.

That was why, when Remond became a founder of the first antislavery society, he joined not only to free the slave, but to free the "free" Negro, too. In 1838 he became one of the many abolitionist lecturers who brought the freedom message to the country. As the most famous Negro in the United States (until the rise of Frederick Douglass), he went abroad to enlist Europe's help in the antislavery crusade.

Across the sea, abolitionists were honored by royalty and workingman alike. Here at home, they were insulted, mobbed, tarred-and-feathered. Their meetings were broken up, their homes sacked, their literature burned, their presses destroyed. But still men like Remond—and there were hundreds of them, Negro and white—persisted. They stood up in pulpits, on platforms, on street corners, in barns, in parlors, in fields, wherever two or three or a thousand could be gathered to hear them. They flung questions to their listeners, they issued challenges, they mocked myths, they demolished lies. And sometimes they made people think. If a man began to think about the prejudices he had taken for granted, he was never the same again.

Once, Remond was asked to speak to the children of the Reverend Samuel J. May's parish. Since May was a noted abolitionist himself, Remond met an unusual situation, which he described in a letter to William Lloyd Garrison's Liberator.

Mothers are the
first book read . . .
1842

MY VERY DEAR FRIEND MR. GARRISON:

I went immediately to the meeting-house, where I found a large audience assembled, and the children of Mr. May's parish engaged in reciting anti-slavery pieces, with which, I was informed, they had, in a very short time, made themselves acquainted; and my only regret was, that there were not thousands present from a distance to witness for themselves the highly interesting occasion.

Many of the pieces were new to me, and never in my life have I seen a juvenile association acquit themselves more creditably. Among the pieces recited, familiar to me, was our friend J. G. Whittier's stanzas, "Our fellow countrymen in chains," "The Yankee Girl," two or three very pertinent dialogues, the letter of Dr. Rushton to General Washington, etc. The services continued about three hours.

At the close of the recitations, I was requested, by friend

May, to offer a few remarks; and I frankly confessed the scene was so new in kind and character in our pro-slavery country, that I scarcely knew how to express myself. However, I could not withhold the expression of my thanks, in behalf of the enslaved, to their friend Mr. May, for interesting the children in the worthy cause of suffering millions—and to the parents and friends, for the encouragement they had given by their presence.

And what a burning shame it is, that many of the pieces on the subject of slavery and the slave-trade, contained in different school books, have been lost sight of, or been subject to the pruning knife of the slaveholding expurgatorial system! To make me believe that those men, or bodies of men, who have regulated the educational institutions of our country, have humanity in their hearts, is to make me believe a lie; and not less so, in making me believe those Christian ministers who profess to love God in words, and hate their brother in works.

I ask, if school committees and school-masters,—if Christian synods, conventions, ministers and Sabbath-school teachers had resolved and taught, preached and prayed for the proscribed and enslaved colored men, women and children, we should at this time find the rising generation shrinking from the mention of their name—repelling them from the lyceum and lecture room—scouting them from the museum and picture gallery—denying them admission to the white schools, seminaries and colleges—spurning them from the cabin on shipboard, and from artisanship and mechanism on land?

I opine otherwise. "Judicious mothers will always keep in mind, that they are the first book read, and the last put aside, in every child's library: every look, word, tone and gesture,

nay, even dress, makes an impression." [*Abbot's Magazine.*]
And what is true of mothers, I believe also true of fathers,
teachers and ministers. I therefore repeat the expression of my
gratitude to our long tried friend May, for the excellent example he has set, while I cannot but exclaim, "Shame on the
cant and hypocrisy of those who can teach virtue, preach
righteousness, and pray blessings for those only, with skins
colored like their own."

Your obliged friend,
C. LENOX REMOND

From *The Mind of the Negro As Reflected in Letters Written
During the Crisis, 1800-1860,* edited by Carter G. Woodson, 1926.

W*hat was slavery like as a way of living? By the 1830's, ex-slaves, freed or runaway, were beginning to tell their stories in print. Many were very widely read. Their fascinating details and dramatic adventures carried a powerful antislavery message. The narrative of Josiah Henson so impressed Harriet Beecher Stowe that when she wrote her novel,* Uncle Tom's Cabin, *Henson was the model for her hero.*

Solomon Northup, a free Negro of New York, was kidnapped in Washington in 1841 and forced into slavery on a cotton plantation near the Red River in Louisiana. Freed in 1853, his story of slavery was recorded in Twelve Years a Slave. *From it is drawn this vivid picture of a slave auction.*

A slave auction . . .

1841

IN THE FIRST PLACE we were re-
quired to wash thoroughly, and those with beards to shave. We
were then furnished with a new suit each, cheap, but clean.
The men had hat, coat, shirt, pants and shoes; the women
frocks of calico, and handkerchief to bind about their heads.
We were now conducted into a large room in the front part of
the building to which the yard was attached, in order to be
properly trained, before the admission of customers. The men
were arranged on one side of the room, the women at the other.
The tallest was placed at the head of the row, then the next
tallest, and so on in the order of their respective heights. Emily
was at the foot of the line of women. Freeman [owner of the
slave-pen] charged us to remember our places; exhorted us to
appear smart and lively,—sometimes threatening, and again,
holding out various inducements. During the day he exercised
us in the art of "looking smart," and of moving to our places
with exact precision.

After being fed, in the afternoon, we were again paraded and made to dance. Bob, a colored boy, who had some time belonged to Freeman, played on the violin. Standing near him, I made bold to inquire if he could play the "Virginia Reel." He answered he could not, and asked me if I could play. Replying in the affirmative, he handed me the violin. I struck up a tune, and finished it. Freeman ordered me to continue playing, and seemed well pleased, telling Bob that I far excelled him—a remark that seemed to grieve my musical companion very much.

Next day many customers called to examine Freeman's "new lot." The latter gentleman was very loquacious, dwelling at much length upon our several good points and qualities. He would make us hold up our heads, walk briskly back and forth, while customers would feel of our hands and arms and bodies, turn us about, ask us what we could do, make us open our mouths and show our teeth, precisely as a jockey examines a horse which he is about to barter for or purchase. Sometimes a man or woman was taken back to the small house in the yard, stripped, and inspected more minutely. Scars upon a slave's back were considered evidence of a rebellious or unruly spirit, and hurt his sale.

An old gentleman, who said he wanted a coachman, appeared to take a fancy to me . . . . I learned he was a resident in the city. I very much desired that he would buy me, because I conceived it would not be difficult to make my escape from New Orleans on some northern vessel. Freeman asked him fifteen hundred dollars for me. The old gentleman insisted it was too much as times were very hard. Freeman, however, declared that I was sound of health, of a good constitution, and intelligent. He made it a point to enlarge upon my musical attainments. The old gentleman argued quite adroitly that there was nothing extraordinary about the Negro, and finally, to my regret, went out, saying he would call again.

During the day, however, a number of sales were made. David and Caroline were purchased together by a Natchez planter. They left us, grinning broadly, and in a most happy state of mind, caused by the fact of their not being separated. Sethe was sold to a planter of Baton Rouge, her eyes flashing with anger as she was led away.

The same man also purchased Randall. The little fellow was made to jump, and run across the floor, and perform many other feats, exhibiting his activity and condition. All the time the trade was going on, Eliza was crying aloud, and wringing her hands. She besought the man not to buy him, unless he also bought herself and Emily. She promised, in that case, to be the most faithful slave that ever lived. The man answered that he could not afford it, and then Eliza burst into a paroxysm of grief, weeping plaintively. Freeman turned round to her, savagely, with his whip in his uplifted hand, ordering her to stop her noise, or he would flog her. He would not have such work —such snivelling; and unless she ceased that minute, he would take her to the yard and give her a hundred lashes. Yes, he would take the nonsense out of her pretty quick—if he didn't might he be d——d. Eliza shrunk before him, and tried to wipe away her tears, but it was all in vain. She wanted to be with her children, she said, the little time she had to live.

All the frowns and threats of Freeman could not wholly silence the afflicted mother. She kept on begging and beseeching them, most piteously, not to separate the three. Over and over again she told them how she loved her boy. A great many times she repeated her former promises—how very faithful and obedient she would be; how hard she would labor day and night, to the last moment of her life; if he would only buy them all together. But it was of no avail; the man could not afford it. The bargain was agreed upon, and Randall must go alone. Then Eliza ran to him; embraced him passionately; kissed him again and again; told him to remember her—all the while her tears falling in the boy's face like rain.

Freeman damned her, calling her a blubbering, bawling wench, and ordered her to go to her place, and behave herself, and be somebody. He swore he wouldn't stand such stuff but a little longer. He would soon give her something to cry about, if she was not mighty careful, and that she might depend upon.

The planter from Baton Rouge, with his new purchase, was ready to depart.

"Don't cry, mama. I will be a good boy. Don't cry," said Randall, looking back, as they passed out of the door.

What has become of the lad, God knows. It was a mournful scene indeed. I would have cried myself if I had dared.

From *Twelve Years a Slave,* by Solomon Northup, 1853.

TWENTY-EIGHTH THOUSAND

TWELVE YEARS A SLAVE.

—

NARRATIVE

OF

SOLOMON NORTHUP,

A CITIZEN OF NEW-YORK,

KIDNAPPED IN WASHINGTON CITY IN 1841,

AND

RESCUED IN 1853,

FROM A COTTON PLANTATION NEAR THE RED RIVER,
IN LOUISIANA.

NEW YORK:
MILLER, ORTON & MULLIGAN,
25 PARK ROW, OPPOSITE ASTOR HOUSE.
AUBURN:
107 GENESEE STREET.
1855.

Working *"from day clean to first dark"* under the overseer or his drivers was the usual routine for the slave. It was natural for him to give as little as possible of his unpaid toil, and equally natural for the slaveholder to try to get as much as he could out of his bondsmen.

Most masters let their slaves rest and relax on Sundays, and some gave half of Saturdays, too. Special holidays were few—Good Friday, Independence Day, Christmas. To celebrate the last, there were often two or three days, with gifts and feasts and passes to visit. The fugitive slave, Solomon Northup, left this record of Christmas on a Louisiana plantation.

Christmas on the plantation . . .

1841

THE ONLY RESPITE from constant labor the slave has through the whole year, is during the Christmas holidays. Epps allowed us three—others allow four, five and six days, according to the measure of their generosity. It is the only time to which they look forward with any interest or pleasure. They are glad when night comes, not only because it brings them a few hours repose, but because it brings them one day nearer Christmas. It is hailed with equal delight by the old and the young; even Uncle Abram ceases to glorify Andrew Jackson, and Patsy forgets her many sorrows, amid the general hilarity of the holidays. It is the time of feasting, and frolicking, and fiddling—the carnival season with the children of bondage. They are the only days when they are allowed a little restricted liberty, and heartily indeed do they enjoy it.

It is custom for one planter to give a "Christmas supper," inviting the slaves from neighboring plantations to join his own on the occasion; for instance, one year it is given by Epps, the next by Marshall, the next by Hawkins, and so on. Usually from three to five hundred are assembled, coming together on foot, in carts, on horseback, on mules, riding double and triple, sometimes a boy and girl, an old woman. Uncle Abram astride a mule, with Aunt Phebe and Patsy behind him, trotting towards a Christmas supper, would be no uncommon sight on Bayou Boeuf.

Then, too, "of all days i' the year," they array themselves in their best attire. The cotton coat has been washed clean, the stump of a tallow candle has been applied to their shoes, and if so fortunate as to possess a rimless or a crownless hat, it is placed jauntily on the head. They are welcome with equal cordiality, however, if they come bare-headed and bare-footed to the feast. As a general thing, the women wear handkerchiefs tied about their heads, but if chance has thrown in their way a fiery red ribbon, or a cast-off bonnet of their mistress' grandmother, it is sure to be worn on such occasions. Red—the deep blood red—is decidedly the favorite color among the enslaved damsels of my acquaintance. If a red ribbon does not encircle the neck, you will be certain to find all the hair of their woolly heads tied up with red strings of one sort or another.

The table is spread in the open air, and loaded with varieties of meat and piles of vegetables. Bacon and corn meal at such times are dispensed with. Sometimes the cooking is performed in the kitchen on the plantation, at others in the shade of wide branching trees. In the latter case, a ditch is dug in the ground, and wood laid in and burned until it is filled with glowing coals, over which chickens, ducks, turkeys, pigs, and not unfrequently the entire body of a wild ox, are roasted. They are furnished also with flour, of which biscuits are made, and often with peach and other preserves, with tarts, and every manner and description of pies, except the mince, that being an article of pastry as yet unknown among them. Only the slave who has lived all the years on his scanty allowance of meal and bacon, can appreciate such suppers. White people in great numbers assemble to witness the gastronomical enjoyments . . . .

When the viands have disappeared, and the hungry maws of the children of toil are satisfied, then, next in the order of amusement, is the Christmas dance. My business on these gala days always was to play on the violin. The African race is a music-loving one, proverbially; and many there were among my fellow-bondsmen whose organs of tune were strikingly developed, and who could thumb the banjo with dexterity . . . .

On that particular Christmas I have now in my mind, Miss Lively and Mr. Sam, the first belonging to Stewart, the latter to Roberts, started the ball. It was well known that Sam cherished an ardent passion for Lively, as also did one of Marshall's and another of Carey's boys; for Lively was lively indeed, and a heart-breaking coquette withal. It was a victory for Sam Roberts, when, rising from the repast, she gave him her hand for the first "figure" in preference to either of his rivals. They were somewhat crest-fallen, and, shaking their heads angrily, rather intimated they would like to pitch into Mr. Sam and hurt him badly.

But not an emotion of wrath ruffled the placid bosom of Samuel as his legs flew like drum-sticks down the outside and up the middle, by the side of his bewitching partner. The whole company cheered them vociferously, and, excited with the applause, they continued "tearing down" after all the others had become exhausted and halted a moment to recover breath. But

Sam's superhuman exertions overcame him finally, leaving Lively alone, yet whirling like a top. Thereupon one of Sam's rivals, Pete Marshall, dashed in, and, with might and main, leaped and shuffled and threw himself into every conceivable shape, as if determined to show Miss Lively and all the world that Sam Roberts was of no account . . . .

One "set" off, another takes its place, he or she remaining longest on the floor receiving the most uproarious commendation, and so the dancing continues until broad daylight. It does not cease with the sound of the fiddle, but in that case they set up a music peculiar to themselves. This is called "patting," accompanied with one of those unmeaning songs, composed rather for its adaption to a certain tune or measure, than for the purpose of expressing any distinct idea. The patting is performed by striking the hands on the knees, then striking the hands together, then striking the right shoulder with one hand, the left with the other—all the while keeping time with the feet, and singing, perhaps this song:

> *Harper's creek and roarin' ribber,*
> *Thar, my dear, we'll live forebber;*
> *Den we'll go to de Ingin nation,*
> *All I want in dis creation,*
> *Is pretty little wife and big plantation*

Or, if these words are not adapted to the tune called for, it may be that *Old Hog Eye* is—a rather solemn and startling specimen of versification, not, however, to be appreciated unless heard at the South. It runneth as follows:

> *Who's been here since I've been gone?*
> *Pretty little girl wid a josey on.*

Hog Eye!
Old Hog Eye!
And Hosey too!
Never see de like since I was born,
Here comes a little gal wid a josey on.
Hog Eye!
Old Hog Eye!
And Hosey too!

During the remaining holidays succeeding Christmas, they are provided with passes, and permitted to go where they please within a limited distance, or they may remain and labor on the plantation, in which case they are paid for it. It is very rarely, however, that the latter alternative is accepted. They may be seen at these times hurrying in all directions, as happy looking mortals as can be found on the face of the earth. They are different beings from what they are in the field; the temporary relaxation, the brief deliverance from fear, and from the lash, producing an entire metamorphosis in their appearance and demeanor. In visiting, riding, renewing old friendships, or, perchance, reviving some old attachment, or pursuing whatever pleasure may suggest itself, the time is occupied.

Such is "southern life as it is," three days in the year, as I found it—the other three hundred and sixty-two being days of weariness, and fear, and suffering, and unremitting labor.

From *Twelve Years a Slave,* by Solomon Northup, 1853.

4 mo. 14 - 1844 — John Osborn and wife and two children from Maysville Kentucky — 0 = 4

5 mo 8 : A colored man and wife from Mason Co. Kentucky &c - 2

5 mo 10 A colored man from Winchester Kentucky

5 mo 25 = 4 colored men from Mason Co. Kentucky, one of them taken in Woodbury by that tobacco pedler — ... 4

5 mo. 27 3 colored men — D.W. from Mason Co Kentucky 3

6 mo 3 2 colored men from Hentin Co. Kentucky — 0 2

Everyone who knows *Uncle Tom's Cabin* remembers how the fugitive slave Eliza crossed the ice on the Ohio River to freedom on the other side.

There was a real Eliza who crossed the Ohio early in the 1830's, giving Harriet Beecher Stowe the idea for that incident. Eliza was welcomed at the house of John Rankin, a Tennessee minister who made his home on the riverbank, one of the most important stations on the Underground Railroad.

The "railroad" was a term for the series of stopping points that ran northward along many paths. The slave's friends—

black and white—gave him food and a bed for the night and started him toward the next station. Thousands of brave men and women defied the federal fugitive slave laws to operate the Underground Railroad.

Some of the "conductors" aided great numbers to escape. Levi Coffin and Thomas Garret, white Quakers, each speeded almost three thousand runaways. Robert Purvis and William Still, Philadelphia Negroes, were said to have helped nine thousand fugitives.

There were conductors at the Southern end, too, and most of them were Negroes. Josiah Henson brought out a hundred people, and Harriet Tubman, called "Moses," went down deep into "Egypt-land" nineteen times to rescue over three hundred slaves.

Because of the secrecy required to make the passage North safe, few records were left of the operation. One of these is a letter from the fugitive slave, J. H. Hill, telling how he was helped to escape from Virginia in 1853.

On the Underground Railroad ...

1853

NINE MONTHS I was trying to get away. I was secreted for a long time in a kitchen of a merchant near the corner of Franklyn and 7th streets, at Richmond, where I was well taken care of, by a lady friend of my mother. When I got tired of staying in that place, I wrote myself a pass to pass myself to Petersburg, here I stopped with a very prominent colored person, who was a friend to freedom—stayed here until two white friends told other friends if I was in the city to tell me to go at once, and stand not upon the order of going, because they had heard a plot.

I wrote a pass, started for Richmond, reached Manchester, got off the cars walked into Richmond, once more got back into the same old den, stayed here from the 16th of Aug. to 12th Sept. [1853]. On the 11th of Sept. 8 o'clock P.M. a message came to me that there had been a state room taken on the steamer *City of Richmond* for my benefit, and I assured the party that it would be occupied if God be willing.

Before 10 o'clock the next morning, on the 12th, a beautiful Sept. day, I arose early, wrote my pass for Norfolk left my old den with a many a good bye, turned out the back way to 7th St., thence to Main, down Main behind 4 night watch to old Rockett's and after about 20 minutes of delay I succeeded in reaching the state room. My conductor was very much excited, but I felt as composed as I do at this moment, for I had started from my den that morning for liberty or for death providing myself with a brace of pistols.

From *The Underground Railroad,* by William Still, 1878.

S*laveowners whose "property"*
disappeared in the night went to great trouble to track down
the fugitives. A healthy slave was worth a good deal of money
and his loss was painful. Thousands of men and women, usu-
ally young, fled annually. No greater proof of how much bond-
age was hated could be offered, but nevertheless Dr. Samuel
Cartwright of Louisiana published his theory that there was
a disease peculiar to Negroes called "drapetomania—the dis-
ease causing Negroes to run away." It must have been a power-
ful infection, for it overcame all remedies concocted to prevent
it.

One of the "diseased" slaves was Henry Bibb, who ran away
because he could not bear to see his wife and child flogged,
yet could do nothing to prevent it. Free, he might be able to
carry them off later, or to buy their freedom. His Kentucky
owner learned the fugitive's address and wrote to him. In 1844
Bibb replied from Detroit.

The runaway "disease" . . .

1844

DEAR SIR:—I am happy to inform you that you are not mistaken in the man whom you sold as property, and received pay for as such. But I thank God that I am not property now, but am regarded as a man like yourself, and although I live far north, I am enjoying a comfortable living by my own industry. If you should ever chance to be traveling this way, and will call on me, I will use you better than you did me while you held me as a slave. Think not that I have any malice against you, for the cruel treatment which you inflicted on me while I was in your power. As it was the custom of your country, to treat your fellow men as you did me and my little family, I can freely forgive you.

I wish to be remembered in love to my aged mother, and friends; please tell her that if we should never meet again in this life, my prayer shall be to God that we may meet in Heaven, where parting shall be no more.

You wish to be remembered to King and Jack. I am pleased,

sir, to inform you that they are both here, well, and doing well. They are both living in Canada West. They are now the owners of better farms than the men are who once owned them.

You may perhaps think hard of us for running away from slavery, but as to myself, I have but one apology to make for it, which is this: I have only to regret that I did not start at an earlier period. I might have been free long before I was. But you had it in your power to have kept me there much longer than you did. I think it is very probable that I should have been a toiling slave on your property today, if you had treated me differently.

To be compelled to stand by and see you whip and slash my wife without mercy, when I could afford her no protection, not even by offering myself to suffer the lash in her place, was more than I felt it to be the duty of a slave husband to endure, while the way was open to Canada. My infant child was also frequently flogged by Mrs. Gatewood, for crying, until its skin was bruised literally purple. This kind of treatment was what drove me from home and family, to seek a better home for them. But I am willing to forget the past. I should be pleased to hear from you again, on the reception of this, and should also be very happy to correspond with you often, if it should be agreeable to yourself. I subscribe myself a friend to the oppressed, and Liberty forever.

From *Narrative of the Life and Adventures of Henry Bibb, an American Slave*, 1849.

PROCEEDINGS

OF THE

COLORED

NATIONAL CONVENTION,

HELD IN

ROCHESTER, JULY 6TH, 7TH AND 8TH,

1 8 5 3 .

ROCHESTER:
PRINTED AT THE OFFICE OF FREDERICK DOUGLASS' PAPER.
1853.

S*outhern slaveowners were troubled by the problem of what to do about free Negroes. A free Negro was living proof to the slave that bondage was not inevitable. Every runaway showed that "self-emancipation" was* *possible. And many went beyond example: they formed living links on the Underground Railroad, carrying other slaves to freedom.*

One answer to the problem was offered by prominent slaveholders when they formed the American Colonization Society late in 1816. To keep their slave property secure and disciplined, they planned to send free Negroes to a colony in Africa. Funds were raised and agents enlisted to promote the idea among Negroes. But the campaign fizzled. Hardly fifteen thousand left for Liberia over a period of many years.

The Negroes themselves did not want to go. They were not strangers here; this was their own land. In Philadelphia, three thousand Negroes met in 1817 to oppose colonization. That was the first Negro convention. Protests against discrimination and second-class citizenship rose higher and higher. Northern Negroes, able to organize and speak and write publicly in defense of their rights, met again in Philadelphia in 1830. From then on, national Negro conventions met in various Northern cities to combine their forces against slavery and for full citizenship.

From the 1853 convention in Rochester, New York, came blunt words which hammered at the wall of prejudice and persecution surrounding the colored people.

Prejudice exposed . . .

1853

As a people, we feel ourselves to be not only deeply injured, but grossly misunderstood. Our white fellow-countrymen do not know us. They are strangers to our character, ignorant of our capacity, oblivious of our history and progress, and are misinformed as to the principles and ideas that control and guide us as a people. The great mass of American citizens estimate us as being a characterless and purposeless people; and hence we hold up our heads, if at all, against the withering influence of a nation's scorn and contempt.

It will not be surprising that we are so misunderstood and misused when the motives for misrepresenting us and for degrading us are duly considered. Indeed, it will seem strange, upon such consideration (and in view of the ten thousand channels through which malign feelings find utterance and influence), that we have not even fallen lower in public estimation than we have done. For, with the single exception of the

104

Jews, under the whole heavens, there is not to be found a people pursued with a more relentless prejudice and persecution, than are the free colored people of the United States.

Without pretending to have exerted ourselves as we ought, in view of an intelligent understanding of our interest, to avert from us the unfavorable opinions and unfriendly action of the American people, we feel that the imputations cast upon us, for our want of intelligence, morality and exalted character, may be mainly accounted for by the injustice we have received at your hands. What stone has been left unturned to degrade us? What hand has refused to fan the flame of popular prejudice against us? What American artist has not caricatured us? What wit has not laughed at us in our wretchedness? What songster has not made merry over our depressed spirits? What press has not ridiculed and condemned us? What pulpit has withheld from our devoted heads its angry lightning or its sanctimonious hate?

Few, few, very few; and that we have borne up with it all —that we have tried to be wise, though denounced by all to be fools—that we have tried to be upright, when all around us have esteemed us as knaves—that we have striven to be gentlemen, although all around us have been teaching us its impossibility—that we have remained here, when all our neighbors have advised us to leave, proves that we possess qualities of head and heart such as cannot but be commended by impartial men. It is believed that no other nation on the globe could have made more progress in the midst of such an universal and stringent disparagement. It would humble the proudest, crush the energies of the strongest, and retard the progress of the swiftest. In view of our circumstances, we can, without boasting, thank God, and take courage, having placed ourselves where we may fairly challenge comparison with more highly favored men.

Among the colored people we can point, with pride and hope, to men of education and refinement, who have become such, despite of the most unfavorable influences, we can point to mechanics, farmers, merchants, teachers, ministers, doctors, lawyers, editors, and authors against whose progress the concentrated energies of American prejudice have proved quite unavailing.

Now, what is the motive for ignoring and discouraging our improvement in this country? The answer is ready. The intelligent and upright free man of color is an unanswerable argument in favor of liberty, and a killing condemnation of American slavery. It is easily seen that, in proportion to the progress of the free man of color in knowledge, temperance, industry, and righteousness, in just that proportion will he endanger the stability of slavery; hence, all the powers of slavery are exerted to prevent the elevation of the free people of color.

The force of fifteen hundred million dollars is arrayed against us; hence, the press, the pulpit, and the platform, against all the natural promptings of uncontaminated manhood, point their deadly missiles of ridicule, scorn and contempt at us; and bid us, on pain of being pierced through and through, to remain in our degradation.

Let the same amount of money be employed against the interest of any other class of persons, however favored by nature they may be, the result could scarcely be different from that seen in our own case. Such a people would be regarded with aversion; the money-ruled multitude would heap contumely upon them, and money-ruled institutions would proscribe them.

Besides this money consideration, fellow-citizens, an explanation of the erroneous opinions prevalent concerning us is furnished in the fact, less creditable to human nature, that men are apt to hate most those whom they injure most. Having despised us, it is not strange that Americans should seek to render us despicable; having enslaved us, it is natural that they should strive to prove us unfit for freedom; having denounced us as indolent, it is not strange that they should cripple our enterprise; having assumed our inferiority, it would be extraordinary if they sought to surround us with circumstances which would serve to make us direct contradictions to their assumption.

From *Proceedings of the Colored National Convention,*
held in Rochester, July 6-8, 1853.

A free Negro's chance to get an education improved in the North as time went on. But in many places there still were separate schools for Negro children. The Massachusetts abolitionists stopped Jim Crow schools in Boston and New Bedford by 1855. Most other Northern states maintained separate schools much longer. Negroes who migrated to the Midwest generally had to wait until after the Civil War for free public education.

Determined Negroes were not content to wait indefinitely for integration. In Boston, the Negro lawyer Robert Morris teamed with the white Charles Sumner to fight segregation. In Philadelphia, Robert Purvis decided early to dedicate his life and his inherited wealth to ending slavery and discrimina-

tion. The son of a Moorish-Negro woman and a wealthy Englishman, he was born in Charleston, South Carolina, and educated in Edinburgh. He helped to organize the first national Negro convention. At twenty-three, he was one of the founders of the American Anti-Slavery Society, and later became its president. As a leader of the Pennsylvania abolitionists, he organized the Philadelphia Vigilance Committee which guided slave runaways through the city and helped pay their way to Canada. His methods became the pattern for the operation of the Underground Railroad.

Purvis gave unselfishly of his time, energy, and money. He never hesitated at personal danger. On his elegant suburban estate he raised blue-ribbon livestock and poultry and entertained abolitionists seeking a rest or his counsel. It was here that his young niece Charlotte Forten learned her abolitionist principles.

In 1853, refusing to pay the local school tax, Robert Purvis wrote this explanation to the tax collector. It helped end the separation policy of the schools.

A refusal
to pay taxes . . .
1853

YOU CALLED yesterday for the tax
upon my property in this Township, which I shall pay, except-
ing the "School Tax." I object to the payment of this tax, on
the ground that my rights as a citizen, and my feelings as a
man and a parent, have been grossly outraged in depriving me,
in violation of law and justice, of the benefits of the school
system which this tax was designed to sustain.

I am perfectly aware that all that makes up the character
and worth of the citizens of this township look upon the pro-
scription and exclusion of my children from the Public School
as illegal, and an unjustifiable usurpation of my right. I have
borne this outrage ever since the innovation upon the usual
practice of admitting all the children of the Township into the
Public Schools, and at considerable expense have been obliged
to obtain the services of private teachers to instruct my chil-

dren, while my school tax is greater, with a single exception, than that of any other citizen of the township.

It is true (and the outrage is made but the more glaring and insulting), I was informed by a pious Quaker director, with a sanctifying grace, imparting, doubtless, an unctuous glow to his saintly prejudices, that a school in the village of Mechanicsville was appropriated for "thine." The miserable shanty, with all its appurtenances, on the very line of the township, to which this benighted follower of George Fox alluded, is, as you know, the most flimsy and ridiculous sham which any tool of a skin-hating aristocracy could have resorted to, to cover or protect his servility.

To submit by voluntary payment of the demand is too great an outrage upon nature, and, with a spirit, thank God, unshackled by this, or any other wanton and cowardly act, I shall resist this tax, which, before the unjust exclusion, had always afforded me the highest gratification in paying. With no other than the best feeling towards yourself, I am forced to this unpleasant position, in vindication of my rights and personal dignity against an encroachment upon them as contemptibly mean as it is infamously despotic.

From *The Liberator,* December 16, 1853.

Yours truly
J. W. Loguen

J. W. Loguen was the son of a
slave mother and the white man who owned her. His mother
had been born free in Ohio, but when she was seven, she was
kidnapped and sold to a Tennessean who ran a whiskey dis-

112

tillery with slave labor. As soon as he could, the boy rode off to freedom on his master's mare. Fearless and intelligent, he earned his way through college and became a minister in Syracuse, New York. When the Fugitive Slave Law was adopted in 1850, he announced publicly: "I am a fugitive slave from Tennessee. My master is Manasseth Logue. The letter of the law gives him a title to my person—and let him come and take it. I'll not run, nor will I give him a penny for my freedom."

At a meeting held in Syracuse in October, 1850, the Reverend Mr. Loguen made a speech that forecast how militant Negroes would meet the new Fugitive Slave Law. One year later, he proved dramatically that he meant exactly what he said. He took part in the rescue of the runaway slave Jerry, when crowbars and a battering-ram were used to break into the Syracuse courthouse and free the fugitive under the guns of the marshals. The episode was a national sensation. Would force alone end slavery? More and more began to believe it.

Let him come and take me . . .
1850

I WAS A SLAVE; I knew the dangers I was exposed to. I had made up my mind as to the course I was to take. On that score I needed no counsel, nor did the colored citizens generally. They had taken their stand—they would not be taken back to slavery. If to shoot down their assailants should forfeit their lives, such result was the least of the evil. They will have their liberties or die in their defence.

What is life to me if I am to be a slave in Tennessee? My neighbors! I have lived with you many years, and you know me. My home is here, and my children were born here. I am bound to Syracuse by pecuniary interests, and social and family bonds. And do you think I can be taken away from you and from my wife and children, and be a slave in Tennessee? Has the President and his Secretary sent this enactment up here, to you, Mr. Chairman, to enforce on me in Syracuse?—and will you obey him? Did I think so meanly of you—did I suppose the people of Syracuse, strong as they are in numbers and love of liberty—or did I believe their love of liberty was so selfish, unmanly and unchristian—did I believe them so sunken and servile and degraded as to remain at their homes and labors, or, with none of that spirit which smites a tyrant down, to surround a United States Marshal to see me torn from my home and family, and hurled back to bondage—I say did I think so meanly of you, I could never come to live with you . . . .

I tell you the people of Syracuse and of the whole North must meet this tyranny and crush it by force, or be crushed by it. This hellish enactment has precipitated the conclusion that white men must live in dishonorable submission, and colored men be slaves, or they must give their physical as well as intellectual powers to the defence of human rights. The time has come to change the tones of submission into tones of defiance —and to tell Mr. Fillmore and Mr. Webster, if they propose to execute this measure upon us, to send on their blood-hounds.

Mr. President, long ago I was beset by over prudent and good men and women to purchase my freedom. Nay, I was frequently importuned to consent that they purchase it, and present it as an evidence of their partiality to my person and character. Generous and kind as those friends were, my heart recoiled from the proposal. I owe my freedom to the God who made me, and who stirred me to claim it against all other beings in God's universe. I will not, nor will I consent, that anybody else shall countenance the claims of a vulgar despot to my soul and body. Were I in chains, and did these kind people come to buy me out of prison, I would acknowledge the boon with inexpressible thankfulness. But I feel no chains, and am in no prison. I received my freedom from Heaven, and with it came the command to defend my title to it. I have long since resolved to do nothing and suffer nothing that can in any way imply that I am indebted to any power but the Almighty for my manhood and personality.

Now, you are assembled here, the strength of this city is here to express their sense of this fugitive act, and to proclaim to the despots at Washington whether it shall be enforced here—whether you will permit the government to return me and other fugitives who have sought an asylum among you, to the Hell of slavery. The question is with you. If you will give us up, say so, and we will shake the dust from our feet and leave you. But we believe better things. We know you are taken by surprise. The immensity of this meeting testifies to the general consternation that has brought it together, necessarily, precipitately, to decide the most stirring question that can be presented, to wit, whether, the government having transgressed constitutional and natural limits, you will bravely resist its aggressions, and tell its soulless agents that no slave-holder shall make your city and county a hunting field for slaves.

Whatever may be your decision, my ground is taken. I have declared it everywhere. It is known over the State and out of the State—over the line in the North, and over the line in the South. I don't respect this law—I don't fear it—I won't obey it! It outlaws me, and I outlaw it, and the men who attempt to enforce it on me. I place the governmental officials on the ground that they place me. I will not live a slave, and if force is employed to re-enslave me, I shall make preparations to meet the crisis as becomes a man.

If you will stand by me—and I believe you will do it, for your freedom and honor are involved as well as mine—it requires no microscope to see that—I say if you will stand with

116

us in resistance to this measure, you will be the saviours of your country.

Your decision to-night in favor of resistance will give vent to the spirit of liberty, and it will break the bands of party, and shout for joy all over the North. Your example only is needed to be the type of public action in Auburn, and Rochester, and Utica, and Buffalo, and all the West, and eventually in the Atlantic cities. Heaven knows that this act of noble daring will break out somewhere—and may God grant that Syracuse be the honored spot, whence it shall send an earthquake voice through the land!

From *The Rev. J. W. Loguen, As a Slave and As a Freeman.*
A Narrative of Real Life, 1859.

THE

REV. J. W. LOGUEN,

AS

A SLAVE

AND AS

A FREEMAN.

———————◆———————

A NARRATIVE OF REAL LIFE.

SYRACUSE, N. Y.:

J. G. K. TRUAIR & CO., STEREOTYPERS AND PRINTERS,
OFFICE OF THE DAILY JOURNAL.

1859.

Two dozen of the most respectable citizens of Syracuse, New York, were indicted for treason after the rescue of the runaway slave Jerry in 1851. The Reverend J. W. Loguen and eleven other Negroes were among them. (The government's case was dropped a year later.) The risk of going to jail or being taken back into slavery did not halt Loguen. He went boldly about the country, collecting funds to aid slaves, and stirring the people to meet the Fugitive Slave Law with physical resistance, even to shooting any claimant or federal marshal, if need be, to prevent the return of a slave. For years his home in Syracuse was a major station on *the Underground Railroad. He was credited with piloting over fifteen hundred fugitives into the free haven of Canada.*

In 1860, some twenty years after he had fled from slavery, Loguen received a letter from the woman who had owned him in Tennessee. She knew his whereabouts because he had just published a book about his life as slave and freeman. His reply to her, made public in the abolitionist paper, The Liberator, *showed how differently master and slave looked upon life.*

If you had a heart . . .

1860

MRS. SARAH LOGUE: Yours of the 20th of February is duly received, and I thank you for it. It is a long time since I heard from my poor old mother, and I am glad to know that she is yet alive, and, as you say, "as well as common." What that means, I don't know. I wish you had said more about her.

You are a woman; but had you a woman's heart, you never could have insulted a brother by telling him you sold his only remaining brother and sister, because he put himself beyond your power to convert him into money.

You sold my brother and sister, Abe and Ann, and twelve acres of land, you say, because I ran away. Now you have the unutterable meanness to ask me to return and be your miserable chattel, or, in lieu thereof, send you $1000 to enable you to redeem the land, but not to redeem my poor brother and sister! If I were to send you money, it would be to get my brother and sister, and not that you should get land. You say you are a cripple, and doubtless you say it to stir my pity, for you knew

I was susceptible in that direction. I do pity you from the bottom of my heart. Nevertheless, I am indignant beyond the power of words to express, that you should be so sunken and cruel as to tear the hearts I love so much all to pieces; that you should be willing to impale and crucify us all, out of compassion for your foot or leg. Wretched woman! Be it known to you that I value my freedom, to say nothing of my mother, brothers and sisters, more than your whole body; more, indeed, than my own life; more than all the lives of all the slaveholders and tyrants under heaven.

You say you have offers to buy me, and that you shall sell me if I do not send you $1000, and in the same breath and almost in the same sentence, you say, "You know we raised you as we did our own children." Woman, did you raise your own children for the market? Did you raise them for the whipping-post? Did you raise them to be driven off, bound to a coffle in chains? Where are my poor bleeding brothers and sisters? Can you tell? Who was it that sent them off into sugar and cotton fields, to be kicked and cuffed, and whipped, and to groan and die; and where no kin can hear their groans, or attend and sympathize at their dying bed, or follow in their funeral? Wretched woman! Do you say you did not do it? Then I reply, your husband did, and you approved the deed—and the very letter you sent me shows that your heart approves it all. Shame on you!

But, by the way, where is your husband? You don't speak of him. I infer, therefore, that he is dead; that he has gone to his great account, with all his sins against my poor family upon his head. Poor man! gone to meet the spirits of my poor, outraged and murdered people, in a world where Liberty and Justice are Masters.

But you say I am a thief, because I took the old mare along with me. Have you got to learn that I had a better right to the old mare, as you call her, than Manasseth Logue had to me? Is it a greater sin for me to steal his horse, than it was for him to rob my mother's cradle, and steal me? If he and you infer that I forfeit all my rights to you, shall not I infer that you forfeit all your rights to me? Have you got to learn that human rights are mutual and reciprocal, and if you take my liberty and life, you forfeit your own liberty and life? Before God and high heaven, is there a law for one man which is not a law for every other man?

If you or any other speculator on my body and rights, wish to know how I regard my rights, they need but come here, and lay their hands on me to enslave me. Did you think to terrify me by presenting the alternative to give my money to you, or give my body to slavery? Then let me say to you, that I meet the proposition with unutterable scorn and contempt. The proposition is an outrage and an insult. I will not budge one hair's breadth. I will not breathe a shorter breath, even to save me from your persecutions. I stand among a free people, who, I thank God, sympathize with my rights, and the rights of mankind; and if your emissaries and venders come here to re-enslave me, and escape the unshrinking vigor of my own right arm, I trust my strong and brave friends, in this city and State, will be my rescuers and avengers.

Yours, &c.,
J. W. LOGUEN.

From *The Liberator,* April 27, 1860.

Young *America began celebrating the birthday of its national independence almost before the new republic was out of its cradle. Annually the Fourth of July orators thundered tributes to the Founding Fathers and to the Declaration of Independence. Prayers were made, hymns sung, and sermons preached in honor of those who had shed their blood for justice, liberty, and humanity.*

The ex-slave Frederick Douglass was one of the most prominent citizens of Rochester, New York. Here he edited his abolitionist newspaper, The North Star, *and was stationmaster for the Underground Railroad. In 1852, the city honored him with an invitation to deliver the Fourth of July oration. But Douglass was no mouthpiece for dead history. "We have to do with the past," he said, "only as we can make it useful to the present and the future. You have no right to enjoy a child's share in the labor of your fathers, unless your children also are to be blest by your labors." He then went on to fling this challenge from the American Negro.*

123

What is your Fourth of July to me? . . .

1852

FELLOW CITIZENS: Pardon me, and allow me to ask, why am I called upon to speak here today? What have I or those I represent to do with your national independence? Are the great principles of political freedom and of natural justice, embodied in that Declaration of Independence, extended to us? And am I, therefore, called upon to bring our humble offering to the national altar, and to confess the benefits, and express devout gratitude for the blessings resulting from your independence to us? . . .

What to the American slave is your Fourth of July? I answer, a day that reveals to him more than all other days of the year, the gross injustice and cruelty to which he is the constant victim. To him your celebration is a sham; your boasted liberty an unholy license; your national greatness, swelling vanity; your sounds of rejoicing are empty and heartless; your denunciation of tyrants, brass-fronted impudence; your shouts of liberty and equality, hollow mockery; your prayers and hymns, your sermons and thanksgivings, with all your religious parade and solemnity, are to him mere bombast, fraud, deception, impiety, and hypocrisy—a thin veil to cover up crimes which would disgrace a nation of savages. There is not a nation of the earth guilty of practices more shocking and bloody than are the people of these United States at this very hour.

Go where you may, search where you will, roam through all the monarchies and despotisms of the Old World, travel through South America, search out every abuse and when you have found the last, lay your facts by the side of the everyday practices of this nation, and you will say with me that, for revolting barbarity and shameless hypocrisy, America reigns without a rival . . . .

From *The Life and Writings of Frederick Douglass,*
Volume II, edited by Philip S. Foner, 1950.

WM. WELLS BROWN

A*bolitionist lectures did not find every audience hostile. The years of constant agitation won many friends, and events themselves helped powerfully to make the issue clear. The Fugitive Slave Law of 1850, the bloody struggle to make Kansas a free state, the Dred Scott decision, John Brown's raid—all combined to make people see what a danger slavery was to the continuance of American liberty.*

One of the noted Negro abolitionist agents was William

Wells Brown. The slim, handsome man had been hired out by his Missouri master to Elijah Lovejoy, who taught him to read and write. Later, Brown fled slavery and went to work for a Great Lakes captain whose ship carried many fugitives to freedom. Then he became an antislavery lecturer and writer. He wrote for many papers here and abroad, and was the first American Negro to write and publish a novel, as well as histories of the Negro.

In 1857, he described an amusing experience in western Pennsylvania, where farm families came from miles around, in wagons, on horse, on foot, to hear an antislavery talk.

Such music I
never heard . . .
1857

ALTHOUGH SETTLED several years, this seems a comparatively new country, the log cabins of the early settlers still being occupied. To a New Englander, this part of our "glorious Union" appears very strange. The people are generally kind and hospitable, but wonderfully green. But the oddest feature in our meetings is the swarms of little ones. O, the children! I never beheld so many babies in so short a time, since the commencement of my anti-slavery labors. At one meeting last week, I counted twenty-seven babies in their mothers' arms or in their laps. And such music I never before heard. Take an untuned piano, a cornstalk fiddle, a Swiss hurdy-gurdy, and a Scotchman with his bag-pipes, put them all in one room, and set them agoing, and you will have but a faint idea of the juvenile concert we had that evening.

I waited till a late hour before commencing the meeting, with the hope that the little ones would stop; but I waited in vain. After being reminded by the dusty clock on the wall that it was ten minutes past seven, I counted five babies, whose open mouths were sending forth delicious music, and then commenced my lecture. I raised my voice to the highest note, and the little ones and I had it, "which and tother," for some time. At last, I was about giving it up as a bad job, when an elderly gentleman near me said, "Keep on, sir, the babies will get tired bye and bye, and will go to sleep." This encouraged me, and I continued with renewed vigor; and sure enough, a half an hour more, and I realized the advice of the old man; for, as the clock struck eight, I found the babies all asleep, and I master of the field. It is astonishing how little the people out here are disturbed by the noise of the children; but I presume they have become used to it.

Mr. Isaac Brooks, one of the most devoted friends of freedom in this section, met us at Lockport, and took Mr. Powell and Miss Anthony to Linesville, some twenty-five miles, while I remained and lectured a second time. We could not have wished for a more enthusiastic or better attended meeting than we had at Linesville. The place of meeting was a double schoolhouse, with the partition opened, and the two rooms thrown into one. The Baptist church, the only religious building in the town, was shut against us. The Convention commenced on Saturday morning, and continued till Sunday night at half past ten, and was addressed by Miss Anthony, Mr. Powell and myself . . . .

At Linesville, we found another large crop of children. The scene on Sunday beggars description. The house where we held the meeting was jammed in every part, except a small space in the centre of the room where there were no seats. On their mothers' laps lay a dozen or two babies, while five or six who were old enough to run alone were let loose on the unseated spot on the floor. The latter were supplied with various articles to keep them quiet. One had its father's cane; a second a tin horn; a third its mother's bonnet; and a fourth its father's jackknife. One little boy, seven or eight years old, was lying on the floor, nibbling at his younger brother's toes, while the latter lay in its mother's arms, nibbling at something more substantial.

One bright-eyed boy was chasing a dog about the floor; while another, with two caps on his head, was sailing about to the amusement of the other little ones. In different sections of the room were children standing on the tops of the desks, or hanging around their fathers' or mothers' necks. At this juncture, the house looked as if Barnum's baby show had adjourned to our meeting. Miss Anthony seemed very much amused at a little woman in a pink bloomer, seated on the front bench, with her feet, not long enough to reach the floor, hanging down, while a child a few weeks old, in her arms, nibbled away at its dinner.

O, the noise! I will not attempt to describe it. Suffice it to say, that some babies were crowing, some crying, and some snoring, while mothers were resorting to all sorts of means to keep their babies quiet. One was throwing her child up, and catching it; another patting her foot, and another singing "bi-lo-baby." You may guess how difficult it was to be heard in such an assembly. My head aches now, from the great exertion that I made to be heard above the noise of the children. And poor Powell, I pitied him, from the bottom of my heart, for he had not strength to speak to a still audience, to say nothing of such a noisy one as this; and while he was speaking, as if to make the scene more ridiculous, a tall, brawny man walked in, and, the benches being full, seated himself on the stove, which he thought had no fire in it—but he soon found it too peppery for comfort. Just then, a child tumbled from the top of one of the desks, and Mr. Powell made his bow and retired. But they give us rice pudding out here for breakfast, and that gives me strength to meet the babies.

We are to hold meetings at Albion, Lockport, Coneautville, and one other place, the name of which I have forgotten, and then we go to Painesville. The people here are all alive for the Cleveland Convention, and we anticipate a large gathering and a glorious time.

From *The Mind of the Negro As Reflected in Letters Written During the Crisis, 1800-1860,* edited by Carter G. Woodson, 1926.

Frances Ellen Watkins Harper
spent a lonely childhood in Baltimore. She was born a free Negro in that city in 1825. Orphaned early, she was raised by an aunt who sent her to a school for free colored children until she was thirteen. Then she was obliged to earn her own way, making dresses, taking care of children, and all the while trying to learn to write. At twenty-five, she became a schoolteacher, finding work in Ohio and then Pennsylvania. Newspapers and magazines began publishing her poems. Many were on antislavery themes, for she had helped fugitives on the Underground Railroad wherever she was. In 1854 she became a lecturer for the Maine abolitionists. She travelled widely in the North until the Civil War, and then went South to help the freedmen. She was the most popular Negro poet of her time. In 1859, in The Anglo-African magazine, she warned that no virtue lay in making money for its own sake. Gathering riches would not be the Negro's salvation.

Is money the answer? . . .

1859

WHEN WE HAVE a race of men whom this blood-stained government cannot tempt or flatter, who would sternly refuse every office in the nation's gift, from a president down to a tide-waiter, until she shook her hands from complicity in the guilt of cradle plundering and man stealing, then for us the foundations of an historic character will have been laid.

We need men and women whose hearts are the homes of a high and lofty enthusiasm, and a noble devotion to the cause of emancipation, who are ready and willing to lay time, talent and money on the altar of universal freedom.

We have money among us, but how much of it is spent to bring deliverance to our captive brethren? Are our wealthiest men the most liberal sustainers of the Anti-slavery enterprise? Or does the bare fact of their having money really help mould public opinion and reverse its sentiments?

We need what money cannot buy and what affluence is too

beggarly to purchase. Earnest, self sacrificing souls that will stamp themselves not only on the present but the future. Let us not then defer all our noble opportunities till we get rich. And here I am, not aiming to enlist a fanatical crusade against the desire for riches, but I do protest against chaining down the soul, with its Heaven endowed faculties and God given attributes to the one idea of getting money as stepping into power or even gaining our rights in common with others.

The respect that is only bought by gold is not worth much. It is no honor to shake hands politically with men who whip women and steal babies. If this government has no call for our services, no aim for our children, we have the greater need for them to build up a true manhood and womanhood for ourselves.

The important lesson we should learn, and be able to teach, is how to make every gift, whether gold or talent, fortune or genius, subserve the cause of crushed humanity and carry out the greatest idea of the present age, the glorious idea of human brotherhood.

From *The Anglo-African,* May, 1859.

COPELAND'S TRIAL

*F*ive *Negroes were with John Brown's band on that rainy Sunday night of October 16, 1859, when they attacked the federal arsenal at Harpers Ferry in Virginia. Their plan was to capture the town, give arms to the slaves in that region, and spread the revolt through the South. They took the arsenal, but superior troops overwhelmed them. Most of the twenty-two men were killed, a few escaped, and some were captured.*

Two of the Negroes, Dangerfield Newby, forty-four, and Shields Green, twenty-three, had been born slaves. Newby was shot dead in the raid; he left a wife and seven children in slavery. Osborn Perry Anderson, twenty-nine, escaped and fought

135

later in the Civil War. Lewis Sheridan Leary, twenty-four, left a wife and a baby at Oberlin to join Brown's men. He died in the attack.

The fifth Negro, John A. Copeland, Jr., was born of free parents in North Carolina. They moved to Oberlin where he became a student at the college. When his uncle, Lewis Leary, joined John Brown, Copeland enlisted too.

John Brown was tried, and hanged for treason on December 2, 1859. Two weeks later, after trial, both Shields Green and John Copeland were hanged on the same gallows, going to their deaths just as John Brown had, "with the most unflinching firmness," said the reporter for the Associated Press.

In prison, awaiting execution, Copeland wrote to his family these words.

Could I die in a more noble cause? . . .

1859

DEAR PARENTS,—My fate as far as man can seal it is sealed, but let this not occasion you any misery, for remember the cause in which I was engaged, remember that it was a "Holy Cause," one in which men who in every point of view [were] better than I am have suffered and died. Remember that if I must die I die in trying to liberate a few of my poor and oppressed people from my condition of servitude which God in his Holy Writ has hurled his most bitter denunciations against and in which men who were by the color of their faces removed from the direct injurious effect, have already lost their lives and still more remain to meet the same fate which has been by man decided that I must meet . . . .

I am not terrified by the gallows, which I see staring me in the face, and upon which I am soon to stand and suffer death for doing what George Washington was made a hero for doing . . . . For having lent my aid to a general no less brave, and engaged in a cause no less honorable and glorious, I am to suffer death. Washington entered the field to fight for the freedom of the American people—not for the white man alone, but for both black and white. Nor were they white men alone who fought for the freedom of this country. The blood of black men flowed as freely as that of white men . . . . And some of the very last blood shed was that of black men . . . .

It was a sense of the wrongs which we have suffered that promoted the noble but unfortunate Captain Brown and his associates to attempt to give freedom to a small number, at least, of those who are now held by cruel and unjust laws and by no less cruel and unjust men . . . .

And now, dear brother, could I die in a more noble cause? Could I die in a manner and for a cause which would induce true and honest men more to honor me, and the angels more ready to receive me to their happy home of everlasting joy above?

I imagine that I hear you, and all of you, mother, father, sisters, and brothers, say—"No, there is not a cause for which we, with less sorrow, could see you die." Believe me when I tell you, that though shut up in prison and under sentence of death, I have spent more happy hours here, and were it not that I know that the hearts of those to whom I am attached . . . will be filled with sorrow, I would almost as lief die now as at any time, for I feel that I am prepared to meet my Maker . . . .

From *John Brown and His Men,* by Richard J. Hinton, 1894.

I*n the fall of 1861 the Union fleet captured Port Royal harbor off the South Carolina coast and took control of that district and the Sea Islands. The slave-owners had fled inland, leaving about ten thousand slaves who became "contrabands of war" in the hands of the Northern army. Isolated for generations from the rest of the world, the former slaves had been given few chances for education. Lincoln's government decided to send teachers South to demonstrate that the freedmen could be educated and trained to become useful, independent citizens. It was a chance to refute the old argument that Negroes were fit only for slavery. The next spring, fifty-three teachers—all white—arrived from the North, and took their posts on plantations. They taught the former slaves to read and write, distributed clothing, helped the sick, and did all they could to prepare them for new responsibilities.*

Six months later, twenty-four-year-old Charlotte Forten ar-

rived from Philadelphia as the first Negro teacher to join in the experiment to prove Negroes were as capable of self-improvement as whites. She came just as the army had begun to raise a "black regiment" from the young freedmen of the islands. General Rufus Saxton had chosen Colonel Thomas Wentworth Higginson, a Massachusetts abolitionist, to command and train the new Negro troops. Miss Forten was invited to the army camp to watch the ceremony on January 1, 1863, the day the Emancipation Proclamation went into effect.

It was a glorious day! . . .

1863

New-Year's Day, Emancipation Day, was a glorious one to us. General Saxton and Colonel Higginson had invited us to visit the camp of the First Regiment of South Carolina Volunteers on that day, "the greatest day in the nation's history." We enjoyed perfectly the exciting scene on board the steamboat *Flora*. There was an eager, wondering crowd of the freed people, in their holiday attire, with the gayest of headkerchiefs, the whitest of aprons, and the happiest of faces. The band was playing, the flags were streaming, and everybody was talking merrily and feeling happy. The sun shone brightly, and the very waves seemed to partake of the universal gayety, for they danced and sparkled more joyously than ever before. Long before we reached Camp Saxton, we could see the beautiful grove and the ruins of the old fort near it.

Some companies of the First Regiment were drawn up in line under the trees near the landing, ready to receive us. They were a fine, soldierly looking set of men, and their brilliant dress made a splendid appearance among the trees. It was my

141

good fortune to find an old friend among the officers. He took us over the camp and showed us all the arrangements. Everything looked clean and comfortable; much neater, we were told, than in most of the white camps.

An officer told us that he had never seen a regiment in which the men were so honest. "In many other camps," said he, "the Colonel and the rest of us would find it necessary to place a guard before our tents. We never do it here. Our tents are left entirely unguarded, but nothing has ever been touched." We were glad to know that. It is a remarkable fact, when we consider that the men of this regiment have all their lives been slaves; for we all know that Slavery does not tend to make men honest.

The ceremony in honor of Emancipation took place in the beautiful grove of live-oaks adjoining the camp. I wish it were possible to describe fitly the scene which met our eyes, as we sat upon the stand, and looked down on the crowd before us. There were the black soldiers in their blue coats and scarlet pantaloons; the officers of the First Regiment, and of other regiments, in their handsome uniforms; and there were crowds of lookers-on, men, women, and children, of every complexion, grouped in various attitudes, under the moss-hung trees. The faces of all wore a happy, interested look.

The exercises commenced with a prayer by the chaplain of the regiment. An ode, written for the occasion, was then read and sung. President Lincoln's Proclamation of Emancipation was then read, and enthusiastically cheered. The Rev. Mr. French presented Colonel Higginson with two very elegant flags, a gift to the First Regiment, from the Church of the Puritans, in New York. He accompanied them by an appropriate and enthusiastic speech. As Colonel Higginson took the flags, before he had time to reply to the speech, some of the colored people, of their own accord, began to sing,—

> *"My country, 'tis of thee,*
> *Sweet land of liberty,*
> *Of thee we sing!"*

It was a touching and beautiful incident, and sent a thrill through all our hearts. The Colonel was deeply moved by it. He said that reply was far more effective than any speech he could make. But he did make one of those stirring speeches which are "half battles." All hearts swelled with emotion as we listened to his glorious words, "stirring the soul like the sound of a trumpet." His soldiers are warmly attached to him, and he evidently feels toward them all as if they were his children.

General Saxton spoke also, and was received with great enthusiasm. Throughout the morning, repeated cheers were given for him by the regiment, and joined in heartily by all the people. They know him to be one of the best and noblest men in the world. His unfailing kindness and consideration for them, so different from the treatment they have sometimes received at the hands of United States officers, have caused them to have unbounded confidence in him.

At the close of Colonel Higginson's speech, he presented the flags to the color-bearers, Sergeant Rivers and Sergeant Sutton, with an earnest charge, to which they made appropriate replies.

Mrs. Gage uttered some earnest words, and then the regiment sang John Brown's Hallelujah Song.

After the meeting was over, we saw the dress-parade, which was a brilliant and beautiful sight. An officer told us that the men went through the drill remarkably well, and learned the movements with wonderful ease and rapidity. To us it seemed strange as a miracle to see this regiment of blacks, the first mustered into the service of the United States, thus doing itself honor in the sight of officers of other regiments, many of whom doubtless came to scoff. The men afterward had a great feast; ten oxen having been roasted whole, for their especial benefit.

In the evening there was the softest, loveliest moonlight. We were very unwilling to go home; for, besides the attractive society, we knew that the soldiers were to have grand shouts and a general jubilee that night. But the steamboat was coming, and we were obliged to bid a reluctant farewell to Camp Saxton and the hospitable dwellers therein. We walked the deck of the steamer singing patriotic songs, and we agreed that moonlight and water had never looked so beautiful as they did that night.

At Beaufort we took the row-boat for St. Helena. The boatmen as they rowed sang some of their sweetest, wildest hymns. It was a fitting close to such a day. Our hearts were filled with an exceeding great gladness; for although the government had left much undone, we knew that Freedom was surely born in our land that day. It seemed too glorious a good to realize, this beginning of the great work we had so longed for and prayed for. It was a sight never to be forgotten, that crowd of happy black faces from which the shadow of Slavery had forever passed.

"Forever free! forever free!"—those magical words in the President's Proclamation were constantly singing themselves in my soul.

From *The Freedmen's Book,* by L. Maria Child, 1865.

The world outside the South knew little of the slaves' songs until the Jubilee Singers, a group of Fisk University students, went on their first tour in 1871. They brought the moving music North and then across the sea to Europe. The year before, Colonel Thomas Wentworth Higginson had given a chapter of his book, Army Life in a Black Regiment, to the spirituals he had noted down as he heard them sung by the troops he commanded on the Sea Islands. Earlier, in 1864, Charlotte Forten, the young Negro teaching the freedmen's children on St. Helena Island, had collected a few spirituals and printed them in the Atlantic Monthly.

The songs came out of the experience in slavery of the Negro people. Talented individuals with a feeling for rhyme and poetry probably "composed" the songs from the folk storehouse of memories and images. As they were passed on orally, they must have undergone many changes. There is suffering in the spirituals, but more than sorrow. They have power and vitality and in them speaks the deep desire for freedom. They were the Negro's first gift to American culture. Some of these spirituals were especially fitting for the day of emancipation.

Slavery chain done broke at last . . .

1863

NO MORE AUCTION BLOCK

No more auction block for me,
No more, no more,
No more auction block for me,
Many thousand gone.

No more peck of corn for me,
No more, no more,
No more peck of corn for me,
Many thousand gone.

No more pint of salt for me,
No more, no more,
No more pint of salt for me,
Many thousand gone.

No more driver's lash for me,
No more, no more,
No more driver's lash for me,
Many thousand gone.

SLAVERY CHAIN

Slavery chain done broke at last, broke at last, broke at last,
Slavery chain done broke at last,
Going to praise God till I die.

Way down in-a dat valley, praying on my knees;
Told God about my troubles, and to help me ef-a He please.

I did tell him how I suffer, in de dungeon and de chain,
And de days I went with head bowed down, and my broken flesh and pain.

Slavery chain done broke at last, broke at last, broke at last,
Slavery chain done broke at last,
Going to praise God till I die.

I did know my Jesus heard me, 'cause de spirit spoke to me,
And said, "Rise my child, your chillun, and you too shall be free.

"I done 'p'int one mighty captain for to marshal all my hosts,
And to bring my bleeding ones to me, and not one shall be lost."

Slavery chain done broke at last, broke at last, broke at last,
Slavery chain done broke at last,
Going to praise God till I die.

From *The Negro Caravan,* edited by Sterling A. Brown,
Arthur P. Davis, and Ulysses Lee, 1941.

The year 1863 began gloriously
*for the Negro with the Emancipation Proclamation, but as the
months passed the promise turned into a bloody shambles in
city after city in the North. Newspapers opposing Lincoln's
government charged that the costly war was being waged for
worthless Negroes. Millions of free white men were suffering
for ideals only abolitionists held, they said. The fact that Negroes and whites were competing for jobs added to growing
tensions. Many white workers feared that with emancipation
Negroes would come North, causing a reduction in wages or
the loss of jobs for whites. A federal conscription law favoring
the rich man, who could buy his way out of service, was the*

final straw. Negro homes and schools, orphanages and churches were wrecked or burned and many were lynched in riots which erupted over the North.

A Negro citizen of Detroit, caught up in the violence of a mob, wrote this description of that day's riot. His eyewitness account showed the effects of confused governmental policy and bitter popular prejudice.

A riot in Detroit . . .
1863

THE MOB, in its first appearance to me, was a parcel of fellows running up Lafayette street after two or three colored men. They then returned back, and in a short time I saw a tremendous crowd coming up Croghan street on drays, wagons and foot, with kegs of beer on their wagons, and rushed for the prison. Here they crowded thick and heavy. After this, while I was standing on the corner, with half a dozen other gentlemen, a rifle ball came whistling over our heads. After which we heard several shots, but only one ball passing us. In a short time after this there came one fellow down saying, "I am shot in the thigh." And another came with his finger partly shot off. A few minutes after that another ruffian came down, saying: "If we are got to be killed up for Negroes then we will kill every one in this town."

A very little while after this we could hear them speaking up near the jail, and appeared to be drinking, but I was unable to hear what they said. This done, they gave a most fiendish yell and started down Beaubien street. On reaching Croghan street, a couple of houses west on Beaubien street, they commenced throwing, and before they reached my residence, clubs, brick, and missiles of every description flew like hail. Myself and several others were standing on the side-walk, but were compelled to hasten in and close our doors, while the mob passed my house with their clubs and bricks flying into my windows and doors, sweeping out light and sash!

They then approached my door in large numbers, where I stood with my gun, and another friend with an axe, but on seeing us, they fell back. They approached four times determined to enter my door, but I raised my gun at each time and they fell back. In the meantime part of the mob passed on down Beaubien street. After the principal part had passed, I rushed up my stairs looking to see what they were doing, and heard the shattering of windows and slashing of boards. In a few moments I saw them at Whitney Reynolds, a few doors below Lafayette street. Mr. Reynolds is a cooper; had his shop and residence on the same lot, and was the largest colored cooper establishment in the city—employing a number of hands regular.

I could see from the windows men striking with axe, spade, clubs, &c., just as you could see men thrashing wheat. A sight the most revolting, to see innocent men, women and children, all without respect to age or sex, being pounded in the most brutal manner.

Sickened with the sight, I sat down in deep solicitude in relation to what the night would bring forth; for to human appearance it seemed as if Satan was loose, and his children were free to do whatever he might direct without fear of the city authority.

From *A Thrilling Narrative from the Lips of the Sufferers of the Late Detroit Riot,* 1945 (reprinted).

As soon as Fort Sumter was fired upon, the abolitionists tried to make clear to Lincoln and the North that the Union cause would not triumph unless the war was fought to end slavery. It was "freedom for all, or chains for all," they said. From the beginning Frederick Douglass, the powerful spokesman of the Negro, insisted that both slave and free Negroes should be called into service to fight in an army of liberation.

For almost eighteen months there was grave doubt of the course Lincoln was taking on slavery. He seemed to move so slowly, although he never took a step backward. When the Emancipation Proclamation was announced, the friends of freedom around the world knew that the course the abolitionists had advocated was at last to be followed.

The Union Army ranks were opened to Negroes, and through his newspaper, on March 2, 1863, Douglass issued a flaming call, "Men of Color, To Arms!" His own sons, Lewis and Charles, were among the first to respond. The assurances of equal treatment Douglass had been told he could give were not carried out. Negro soldiers suffered unequal pay, allowances, and opportunities throughout the War. They had to fight a double battle, against slavery in the South, and against Jim Crow in the North.

When the Civil War ended, one hundred eighty thousand Negro troops had served in Lincoln's Army and thirty thousand in the Navy. A quarter of a million had helped the military as laborers. To put an end to slavery, thirty-eight thousand Negroes gave their lives in battle.

Men of color,
to arms! . . .
1863

WHEN FIRST THE rebel cannon shattered the walls of Sumter and drove away its starving garrison, I predicted that the war then and there inaugurated would not be fought out entirely by white men. Every month's experience during these weary years has confirmed that opinion. A war undertaken and brazenly carried on for the perpetual enslavement of colored men, calls logically and loudly for colored men to help suppress it. Only a moderate share of sagacity was needed to see that the arm of the slave was the best defense against the arm of the slaveholder. Hence with every reverse to the national arms, with every exulting shout of victory raised by the slaveholding rebels, I have implored the imperiled nation to unchain against her foes her powerful black hand.

Slowly and reluctantly that appeal is beginning to be heeded. Stop not now to complain that it was not heeded sooner . . . .

By every consideration which binds you to your enslaved

fellow-countrymen, and the peace and welfare of your country; by every aspiration which you cherish for the freedom and equality of yourselves and your children; by all the ties of blood and identity which make us one with the brave black men now fighting our battles in Louisiana and in South Carolina, I urge you to fly to arms, and smite with death the power that would bury the government and your liberty in the same hopeless grave.

I wish I could tell you that the State of New York calls you to this high honor. For the moment her constituted authorities are silent on the subject. They will speak by and by, and doubtless on the right side; but we are not compelled to wait for her. We can get at the throat of treason and slavery through the State of Massachusetts. She was first in the War of Independence; first to break the chains of her slaves; first to make the black man equal before the law; first to admit colored children to her common schools, and she was first to answer with her blood the alarm cry of the nation, when its capital was menaced by rebels. You know her patriotic governor, and you know Charles Sumner. I need not add more.

Massachusetts now welcomes you to arms as soldiers. She has but a small colored population from which to recruit. She has full leave of the general government to send one regiment to the war, and she has undertaken to do it. Go quickly and help fill up the first colored regiment from the North. I am authorized to assure you that you will receive the same wages, the same rations, the same equipments, the same protection, the same treatment and the same bounty, secured to the white soldiers. You will be led by able and skillful officers, men who will take especial pride in your efficiency and success. They will be quick to accord to you all the honor you shall merit by your valor, and see that your rights and feelings are respected by other soldiers. I have assured myself on these points, and can speak with authority.

More than twenty years of unswerving devotion to our common cause may give me some humble claim to be trusted at this momentous crisis. I will not argue. To do so implies hesitation and doubt, and you do not hesitate. You do not doubt. The day dawns; the morning star is bright upon the horizon! The iron gate of our prison stands half open. One gallant rush from the North will fling it wide open, while four millions of our brothers and sisters shall march out into liberty. The chance is now given you to end in a day the bondage of centuries, and to rise in one bound from social degradation to the plane of common equality with all other varieties of men.

Remember Denmark Vesey of Charleston; remember Nathaniel Turner of Southampton; remember Shields Green and Copeland, who followed noble John Brown, and fell as glorious martyrs for the cause of the slave. Remember that in a contest with oppression, the Almighty has no attribute which can take sides with oppressors.

The case is before you. This is our golden opportunity. Let us accept it, and forever wipe out the dark reproaches unsparingly hurled against us by our enemies. Let us win for ourselves the gratitude of our country, and the best blessings of our posterity through all time.

From *The Life and Writings of Frederick Douglass,*
Volume III, edited by Philip S. Foner, 1950.

Negro troops met their first major battle test in the storming of Fort Wagner. It was a Confederate stronghold on Morris Island, South Carolina, just six miles away from St. Helena Island where Charlotte Forten was teaching the former slaves.

Placed at the head of the assault was the Massachusetts Fifty-fourth. Not a man of this first Negro regiment to be raised in the free states had held a musket in his hand eighteen weeks before. Without training in storming a fort they were *sent headlong into a badly planned night attack. The Confederate batteries answered with volcanic blasts of shots and shell but the black soldiers climbed up the parapet to a desperate bayonet struggle at the top. Outnumbered and outgunned, they were ordered back after two assaults.*

The Union casualties were great, and the Fifty-fourth bore the heaviest losses in dead and wounded. But the Negro troops had proved their courage and their soldiership.

Letters from the front gave the folks back home some idea of what the Negro troops were going through. One from Lewis Douglass (son of Frederick Douglass) told his sweetheart, Amelia Loguen (daughter of J. W. Loguen), of the battle at Fort Wagner.

A letter from the front . . .

1863

MY DEAR AMELIA:

I have been in two fights, and am unhurt. I am about to go in another I believe tonight. Our men fought well on both occasions. The last was desperate. We charged that terrible battery on Morris island known as Fort Wagner, and were repulsed . . . . De Forest of your city is wounded, George Washington is missing, Jacob Carter is missing, Charles Reason wounded, Charles Whiting, Charles Creamer all wounded.

I escaped unhurt from amidst that perfect hail of shot and shell. It was terrible. I need not particularize, the papers will give a better [account] than I have time to give. My thoughts are with you often, you are as dear as ever, be good to remember it as I no doubt you will. As I said before we are on the eve of another fight and I am very busy and have just snatched a moment to write you. I must necessarily be brief. Should I fall in the next fight killed or wounded I hope I fall with my face to the foe.

This regiment has established its reputation as a fighting regiment, not a man flinched, though it was a trying time. Men fell all around me. A shell would explode and clear a space of twenty feet. Our men would close up again, but it was no use, we had to retreat, which was a very hazardous undertaking. How I got out of that fight alive I cannot tell, but I am here.

My Dear girl I hope again to see you. I must bid you farewell should I be killed. Remember if I die I die in a good cause. I wish we had a hundred thousand colored troops we would put an end to this war.

Good Bye to all. Your own loving—Write soon—

LEWIS

From *The Mind of the Negro As Reflected in Letters Written During the Crisis, 1800-1860,* edited by Carter G. Woodson, 1926.

O*n April 3, 1865, the Confed-*
erate flag fluttered down from the top of the Capitol in Rich-
mond and the Stars and Stripes were run up. Jefferson Davis'
government had fled the city, together with the garrison troops.
Lee's army had begun its last retreat. Six days later the war
would be over. Now Negro soldiers of a Connecticut regi-
ment, proudly wearing their blue uniforms, marched in to oc-
cupy Richmond. As the fires raging in the city were brought
under control, President Lincoln arrived to tour the smoulder-
ing ruins. J. J. Hill, a Negro soldier, watched the reception of
the President and set down what he saw.

161

Lincoln visits Richmond . . .

1865

THE 3D INSTANT President Lincoln visited the city. No triumphal march of a conqueror could have equalled in moral sublimity the humble manner in which he entered Richmond. I was standing on the bank of the James river viewing the scene of desolation when a boat, pulled by twelve sailors, came up the stream. It contained President Lincoln and his son . . . .

In some way the colored people on the bank of the river ascertained that the tall man wearing the black hat was President Lincoln. There was a sudden shout and clapping of hands. I was very much amused at the plight of one officer who had in charge fifty colored men to put to work on the ruined buildings; he found himself alone, for they left work and crowded to see the President.

As he approached I said to a woman, "Madam, there is the man that made you free." She exclaimed, "Is that President Lincoln?" My reply was in the affirmative. She gazed at him with clasped hands and said, "Glory to God. Give Him the praise for his goodness," and she shouted till her voice failed her.

When the President landed there was no carriage near, neither did he wait for one, but leading his son, they walked over a mile to Gen'l. Weitzel's headquarters at Jeff. Davis' mansion, a colored man acting as guide. Six soldiers dressed in blue, with their carbines, were the advanced guards. Next to them came President Lincoln and son, and Admiral Porter, flanked by the other officers right and left. Then came a correspondent, and in the rear were six sailors with carbines. Then followed thousands of people, colored and white. What a spectacle! I never witnessed such rejoicing in all my life. As the President passed along the street the colored people waved their handkerchiefs, hats and bonnets, and expressed their gratitude by shouting repeatedly, "Thank God for his goodness; we have seen his salvation." The white soldiers caught the sound and swelled the numbers, cheering as they marched along.

All could see the President, he was so tall. One woman standing in a doorway as he passed along shouted, "Thank you, dear Jesus, for this sight of the great conqueror." Another one standing by her side clasped her hands and shouted, "Bless the Lamb—Bless the Lamb." Another one threw her bonnet in the air, screaming with all her might, "Thank you, Master Lincoln." A white woman came to a window but turned away, as if it were a disgusting sight. A few white women looking out of an elegant mansion waved their handkerchiefs.

President Lincoln walked in silence, acknowledging the salute of officers and soldiers, and of the citizens, colored and white. It was a man of the people among the people. It was a great deliverer among the delivered. No wonder tears came to his eyes when he looked on the poor colored people who were once slaves, and heard the blessings uttered from thankful hearts and thanks giving to God and Jesus. They were earnest and heartfelt expressions of gratitude to Almighty God, and thousands of colored men in Richmond would have laid down their lives for President Lincoln. After visiting Jeff. Davis' mansion he proceeded to the rebel capitol and from the steps delivered a short speech, and spoke to the colored people as follows:

"In reference to you, colored people, let me say God has made you free. Although you have been deprived of your God-given rights by your so-called masters, you are now as free as I am, and if those that claim to be your superiors do not know that you are free, take the sword and bayonet and teach them that you are—for God created all men free, giving to each the same rights of life, liberty and the pursuit of happiness."

The gratitude and admiration, amounting almost to worship, with which the colored people of Richmond received the President must have deeply touched his heart. He came among the poor unheralded, without pomp or pride, and walked through the streets, as if he were a private citizen more than a great conqueror. He came not with bitterness in his heart, but with the olive leaf of kindness, a friend to elevate sorrow and suffering, and to rebuild what had been destroyed.

From *A Sketch of the 29th Regiment of Connecticut Colored Troops,* by J. J. Hill, 1867.

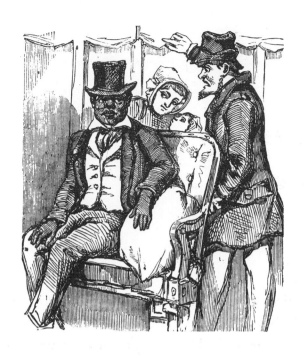

W*hen the government finally permitted Negroes to fight for their own freedom, Philadelphia alone contributed a dozen regiments to the Union army. As the Civil War neared its end, fifteen hundred of these soldiers, wounded in battle, lay in hospitals on the edge of Philadelphia. But their families and friends had great trouble visiting them because the city's passenger cars would not allow colored people to ride.*

In a letter to the Philadelphia Press, *three men tell what happened to them in March, 1865. A year later, continuous protests succeeded in breaking the Jim Crow rules.*

165

No colored
can ride . . .
1865

ON LAST SATURDAY afternoon about 5 o'clock, during a pelting cold rain, we three having an order to attend to in the eastern part of the city, were naturally impressed with the idea that just now, when the impartial draft is making no distinction of color, and when, too, the tax-collectors come to our places of business as readily as to those of white persons, we might be permitted and did enter a car of the Walnut and Chestnut street lines (to avoid the severity of the weather).

But scarcely had we reached the threshold ere we were told by the conductor, "You cannot ride in this car." "Why can we not?" one of us asked. "Because you are not allowed," answered the conductor. "You can draft us in the service, and why can we not ride?" "I do not care for that: you have to go out of this car." "We do not mean to go out; you can put us out if you choose. We came from Boston; we could ride in the cars there; we cannot see why we should not ride here," one of us remarked.

In the meantime a passenger in an excited manner and with harsh language said: "You know you are not allowed to ride in here." "If we are offensive to the passengers we will get up and go out," we said. "You are offensive to these ladies," he responded, in a rage. The ladies rose (but two were in the car), and said emphatically, "They are not offensive, but we want no disturbance."

At this juncture, the conductor called a policeman, who said, "You must leave the car, or be locked up." "Is it against the law for us to ride in here?" we asked. "It is," said the policeman. "Then we will go out," one of us remarked. Another not agreeable to this mandate, said, "It is not against the law, and you may lock me up." "Then I will take you first," said the officer, grabbing him by the collar roughly. "Do you want assistance?" asked the man who first interfered. "Yes," said the officer. At this moment, a regular assault was made upon us by the opposing party, whose numbers had been swelled from without by those who evidently would rather sustain slavery and prejudice than freedom and justice.

Feeling ourselves, however, to be men and not dogs, one of us determined to suffer risk of personal injury and the lock-up rather than run. He came in for more than a due proportion of blows, as fists and the billy were applied freely to his person, the head not being spared. We confess that in the excitement of the moment, we felt unwilling to endure the outrage without resentment, and at least one of us dealt a few blows in return. But we were overpowered and taken before an alderman. Here insult was, as it were, added to injury, for grave charges were made against us; and we soon found that we should be sent to the lock-up unless bail could be procured.

For the time being, our minds were so much absorbed by reflection upon the outrages heaped upon us that we were not in a condition to think of this; hence we were incarcerated, as threatened, and remained so until a friend kindly came and procured our release. These, Mr. Editor, are the simple facts of the case, as they occurred. Without comment, we present them for the consideration of the public.

We try to forget, sir, but we remember that the Democratic cities of New York, Baltimore, Washington, and even New Orleans, do not object to respectable colored persons riding in the cars, while the Republican city of Philadelphia excludes all of her own citizens for color alone.

MILES R. ROBINSON
JAMES WALLACE
R. C. MARSHALL

From *The Liberator,* March 24, 1865.

When the war ended, the South
was a wreck. Its cities were shelled and burned, its fields and
crops ruined, its men dead or wounded. The freed slaves wan-
dered over the land, desperately trying to survive without the
help of masters upon whom they had depended all their lives.
Food for the table, a roof overhead, education for the children,
care for the old folks, work, jobs—where would it come from,
in a desolate and bitter South?

Thousands and thousands of Negroes had left their old
places, sometimes because they wanted something different,
someplace else, whatever it might be. Sometimes because no
one was left to take over things. Sometimes because old masters had returned but had driven them off. One ex-slaveholder,
typical of many, tried to get back a former slave who had
slipped away to freedom during the war. Here is the freed-
man's reply.

To my old master . . .
1865

To my old Master, Colonel P. H. Anderson,
Big Spring, Tennessee.

SIR: I got your letter, and was glad to find that you had not forgotten Jourdon, and that you wanted me to come back and live with you again, promising to do better for me than anybody else can. I have often felt uneasy about you. I thought the Yankees would have hung you long before this, for harboring Rebs they found at your house. I suppose they never heard about your going to Colonel Martin's to kill the Union soldier that was left by his company in their stable. Although you shot at me twice before I left you, I did not want to hear of your being hurt, and am glad you are still living. It would do me good to go back to the dear old home again, and see Miss Mary and Miss Martha and Allen, Esther, Green, and Lee. Give my love to them all, and tell them I hope we will meet in the better world, if not in this. I would have gone back to see you all when I was working in the Nashville Hospital, but one of the neighbors told me that Henry intended to shoot me if he ever got a chance.

I want to know particularly what the good chance is you propose to give me. I am doing tolerably well here. I get twenty-five dollars a month, with victuals and clothing; have a comfortable home for Mandy,—the folks call her Mrs. Anderson,—and the children—Milly, Jane, and Grundy—go to school and are learning well. The teacher says Grundy has a head for a preacher. They go to Sunday school, and Mandy and me attend church regularly. We are kindly treated. Sometimes we overhear others saying, "Them colored people were slaves" down in Tennessee. The children feel hurt when they hear such remarks; but I tell them it was no disgrace in Tennessee to belong to Colonel Anderson. Many darkeys would have been proud, as I used to be, to call you master. Now if you will write and say what wages you will give me, I will be better able to decide whether it would be to my advantage to move back again.

As to my freedom, which you say I can have, there is nothing to be gained on that score, as I got my free papers in 1864 from the Provost-Marshal-General of the Department of Nashville. Mandy says she would be afraid to go back without some proof that you were disposed to treat us justly and kindly; and we have concluded to test your sincerity by asking you to send us our wages for the time we served you. This will make us forget and forgive old scores, and rely on your justice and friendship in the future. I served you faithfully for thirty-two years, and Mandy twenty years. At twenty-five dollars a month for me, and two dollars a week for Mandy, our earnings would amount to eleven thousand six hundred and eighty dollars. Add to this the interest for the time our wages have been kept back, and deduct what you paid for our clothing, and three doctor's visits to me, and pulling a tooth for Mandy, and the balance will show what we are in justice entitled to. Please send the money by Adam's Express, in care of V. Winters, Esq., Dayton, Ohio. If you fail to pay us for faithful labors in the past, we can have little faith in your promises in the future. We trust the good Maker has opened your eyes to the wrongs which you and your fathers have done to me and my fathers, in making us toil for you for generations without recompense. Here I draw my wages every Saturday night; but in Tennessee there was never any pay-day for the Negroes any more than for the horses and cows. Surely there will be a day of reckoning for those who defraud the laborer of his hire.

In answering this letter, please state if there would be any safety for my Milly and Jane, who are now grown up, and both good-looking girls. You know how it was with poor Matilda and Catherine. I would rather stay here and starve—and die, if it come to that—than have my girls brought to shame by the violence and wickedness of their young masters. You will also please state if there has been any schools opened for the colored children in your neighborhood. The great desire of my life now is to give my children an education, and have them form virtuous habits.

Say howdy to George Carter, and thank him for taking the pistol from you when you were shooting at me.

From your old servant,
JOURDON ANDERSON

From *The Freedmen's Book,* by L. Maria Child, 1865.

L ord, Lord, honey!" said Jenny
Proctor. "It seems impossible that any of us ever lived to see
that day of freedom, but thank God we did."

The ex-slave must have been in her nineties when she told
her story to one of the interviewers of the Federal Writers'
Project. That great day of freedom was more than seventy
years gone, but she could still remember how she heard about
it and what she and the other slaves did.

With freedom came great hardship for most of the ex-slaves.
But no matter, said one of them. Anybody who says that he
would rather be slave than free "is telling a lie. There is something 'bout being free, and that makes up for all the hardships.
I's been both slave and free, and I knows."

As Jenny Proctor speaks, calling up the memories of what
she endured on an Alabama farm, she brings home to us what
freedom meant when it finally came.

We was a-gitting going now . . .

I'S HEAR TELL of them good slave days, but I ain't never seen no good times then. My mother's name was Lisa, and when I was a very small child I hear that driver going from cabin to cabin as early as 3 o'clock in the morning, and when he comes to our cabin he say, "Lisa, Lisa, git up from there and git that breakfast." My mother, she was cook, and I don't recollect nothing 'bout my father. If I had any brothers and sisters I didn't know it. We had old ragged huts made out of poles and some of the cracks chinked up with mud and moss and some of them wasn't. We didn't have no good beds, just scaffolds nailed up to the wall out of poles and the old ragged bedding throwed on them. That sure was hard sleeping, but even that feel good to our weary bones after them long hard days' work in the field. I 'tended to the children when I was a little gal and tried to clean the house just like Old Miss tells me to. Then soon as I was ten years old, Old Master, he say, "Git this here nigger to that cotton patch."

I recollects once when I was trying to clean the house like Old Miss tell me, I finds a biscuit, and I's so hungry I et it, 'cause we never see such a thing as a biscuit only sometimes on Sunday morning. We just have corn bread and syrup and sometimes fat bacon, but when I et that biscuit and she comes in and say, "Where that biscuit?" I say, "Miss, I et it 'cause I's so hungry." Then she grab that broom and start to beating me over the head with it and calling me low-down nigger, and I guess I just clean lost my head 'cause I knowed better than to fight her if I knowed anything 't all, but I start to fight her, and the driver, he comes in and he grabs me and starts beating me with that cat-o'-nine-tails, and he beats me till I fall to the floor nearly dead. He cut my back all to pieces, then they rubs salt in the cuts for more punishment. Lord, Lord, honey! Them was awful days. When Old Master come to the house, he say, "What you beat that nigger like that for?" And the driver tells him why, and he say, "She can't work now for a week. She pay for several biscuits in that time." He sure was mad, and he tell Old Miss she start the whole mess. I still got them scars on my old back right now, just like my grandmother have when she die, and I's a-carrying mine right on to the grave just like she did.

Our master, he wouldn't 'low us to go fishing—he say that too easy on a nigger and wouldn't 'low us to hunt none either—but sometime we slips off a night and catch possums. And when Old Master smells them possums cooking 'way in the night, he wraps up in a white sheet and gits in the chimney corner and scratch on the wall, and when the man in the cabin goes to the door and say, "Who's that?" he say, "It's me, what's ye cooking in there?" and the man say, "I's cooking possum."

He say, "Cook him and bring me the hindquarters and you and the wife and the children eat the rest." We never had no chance to git any rabbits 'cept when we was a-clearing and grubbing the new ground. Then we catch some rabbits, and if they looks good to the white folks they takes them and if they no good the niggers git them. We never had no gardens. Sometimes the slaves git vegetables from the white folks' garden and sometimes they didn't.

Money? Uh-uh! We never seen no money. Guess we'd-a bought something to eat with it if we ever seen any. Fact is, we wouldn't-a knowed hardly how to bought anything, 'cause we didn't know nothing 'bout going to town.

They spinned the cloth what our clothes was made of, and we had straight dresses or slips made of lowell. Sometimes they dye 'em with sumac berries or sweet-gum bark, and sometimes they didn't. On Sunday they make all the children change, and what we wears till we gits our clothes washed was gunny sacks with holes cut for our head and arms. We didn't have no shoes 'cepting some homemade moccasins, and we didn't have them till we was big children. The little children they goes naked till they was big enough to work. They was soon big enough though, 'cording to our master. We had red flannel for winter underclothes. Old Miss she say a sick nigger cost more than the flannel.

Weddings? Uh-uh! We just steps over the broom and we's married. Ha! Ha! Ha!

Old Master he had a good house. The logs was all hewed off smooth-like, and the cracks all fixed with nice chinking, plum 'spectable-looking even to the plank floors. That was something. He didn't have no big plantation, but he keeps 'bout three hundred slaves in them little huts with dirt floors. I thinks he calls it four farms what he had.

Sometimes he would sell some of the slaves off of that big auction block to the highest bidder when he could git enough for one.

When he go to sell a slave, he feed that one good for a few days, then when he goes to put 'em up on the auction block he takes a meat skin and greases all round that nigger's mouth and makes 'em look like they been eating plenty meat and such like and was good and strong and able to work. Sometimes he sell all the babes from the breast, and then again he sell the mothers from the babes and the husbands and the wives, and so on. He wouldn't let 'em holler much when the folks be sold away. He say, "I have you whupped if you don't hush." They sure loved their six children though. They wouldn't want nobody buying them.

We might-a done very well if the old driver hadn't been so mean, but the least little thing we do he beat us for it and put big chains round our ankles and make us work with them on till the blood be cut out all around our ankles. Some of the masters have what they call stockades and puts their heads and feet and arms through holes in a big board out in the hot sun, but our old driver he had a bull pen. That's only thing like a jail he had. When a slave do anything he didn't like, he takes 'em in that bull pen and chains 'em down, face up to the sun, and leaves 'em there till they nearly dies.

None of us was 'lowed to see a book or try to learn. They say we git smarter than they was if we learn anything, but we slips around and gits hold of that Webster's old blue-back speller and we hides it till 'way in the night and then we lights a little pine torch, and studies that spelling book. We learn it too. I can read some now and write a little too.

They wasn't no church for the slaves, but we goes to the white folks' arbor on Sunday evening, and a white man he gits up there to preach to the niggers. He say, "Now I takes my text, which is, Nigger obey your master and your mistress, 'cause what you git from them here in this world am all you ever going to git, 'cause you just like the hogs and the other animals—when you dies you ain't no more, after you been throwed in that hole." I guess we believed that for a while 'cause we didn't have no way finding out different. We didn't see no Bibles.

Sometimes a slave would run away and just live wild in the woods, but most times they catch 'em and beats 'em, then chains 'em down in the sun till they nearly die. The only way any slaves on our farm ever goes anywhere was when the boss sends him to carry some news to another plantation or when we slips off way in the night. Sometimes after all the work was done a bunch would have it made up to slip out down to the creek and dance. We sure have fun when we do that, most times on Saturday night.

All the Christmas we had was Old Master would kill a hog and give us a piece of pork. We thought that was something, and the way Christmas lasted was 'cording to the big sweet-gum backlog what the slaves would cut and put in the fireplace. When that burned out, the Christmas was over. So you know we all keeps a-looking the whole year round for the biggest sweet gum we could find. When we just couldn't find the sweet gum, we git oak, but it wouldn't last long enough, 'bout three days on average, when we didn't have to work. Old

Master he sure pile on them pine knots, gitting that Christmas over so we could git back to work.

We had a few little games we play, like Peep Squirrel Peep, You Can't Catch Me, and such like. We didn't know nothing 'bout no New Year's Day or holidays 'cept Christmas.

We had some corn-shuckings sometimes, but the white folks gits the fun and the nigger gits the work. We didn't have no kind of cotton-pickings 'cept just pick our own cotton. I's can hear them darkies now, going to the cotton patch 'way 'fore day a-singing "Peggy, does you love me now?"

One old man he sing:

> *Saturday night and Sunday too*
> *Young gals on my mind.*
> *Monday morning 'way 'fore day*
> *Old Master got me gwine.*
> *Peggy, does you love me now?*

Then he whoops a sort of nigger holler, what nobody can do just like them old-time darkies, then on he goes:

> *Possum up a 'simmon tree,*
> *Rabbit on the ground.*
> *Lord, Lord, possum,*
> *Shake them 'simmons down.*
> *Peggy, does you love me now?*

> *Rabbit up a gum stump,*
> *Possum up a holler.*
> *Git him out, little boy*
> *And I gives you half a dollar.*
> *Peggy, does you love me now?*

We didn't have much looking after when we git sick. We

had to take the worst stuff in the world for medicine, just so it was cheap. That old blue mess and bitter apple would keep us out all night. Sometimes he have the doctor when he thinks we going to die, 'cause he say he ain't got anyone to lose, then that calomel what that doctor would give us would pretty nigh kill us. Then they keeps all kinds of lead bullets and asafetida balls round our necks, and some carried a rabbit foot with them all the time to keep off evil of any kind.

Lord, Lord, honey! It seems impossible that any of us ever lived to see that day of freedom, but thank God we did.

When Old Master comes down in the cotton patch to tell us 'bout being free, he say, "I hates to tell you, but I knows I's got to—you is free, just as free as me or anybody else what's white." We didn't hardly know what he means. We just sort of huddle round together like scared rabbits, but after we knowed what he mean, didn't many of us go, 'cause we didn't know where to of went. Old Master he say he give us the woods land and half of what we make on it, and we could clear it and work it or starve. Well, we didn't know hardly what to do 'cause he just gives us some old dull hoes and axes to work with; but we all went to work, and as we cut down the trees and the poles he tells us to build the fence round the field and we did, and when we plants the corn and the cotton we just plant all the fence corners full too, and I never seen so much stuff grow in all my born days. Several ears of corn to the stalk, and them big cotton stalks was a-laying over the ground. Some of the old slaves they say they believe the Lord knew something 'bout niggers after all. He lets us put corn in his crib, and then we builds cribs and didn't take long 'fore we could buy some hosses and some mules and some good hogs.

Them mangy hogs what our master give us the first year was plumb good hogs after we grease them and scrub them with lye soap. He just give us the ones he thought was sure to die, but we was a-gitting going now, and 'fore long we was a-building better houses and feeling kind of happy-like.

From *Lay My Burden Down,* edited by B. A. Botkin, University of Chicago Press, 1945.

A CALENDAR
OF NEGRO HISTORY
1619-1865

1619 Twenty Negroes brought to Jamestown, Virginia, on a Dutch ship and sold as servants. The beginning of slavery in the English colonies.

1652 First law against slavery in North America enacted by Rhode Island.

1661 Virginia gives legal recognition to slavery.

1667 Virginia legislates that baptism does not change legal status of slave.

1688 Germantown (Pennsylvania) Friends adopt protest against slavery, the earliest antislavery document in America.

1700 First antislavery tract, *The Selling of Joseph,* by Samuel Sewall.

1705 Virginia slave code holds slaves to be real estate.

1712 Slave revolt in New York City. Pennsylvania prohibits importation of Negroes.

1739 Slave insurrection at Stono, South Carolina.

1758 Philadelphia Friends exclude buyers or sellers of slaves from membership.

1770 Crispus Attucks, Negro seaman, killed by British soldiers in Boston Massacre.

1773 *Poems on Various Subjects,* by Phillis Wheatley, young Boston slave, published in London.

1775 First abolition society in America organized in Philadelphia, with Benjamin Franklin as president.

1776 Continental Congress proclaims the Declaration of Independence. It asserts the rights of man, but does not mention slavery.

1777 Vermont abolishes slave trade.

1778 Virginia abolishes slave trade.

1780 First African Baptist Church founded in Richmond, Virginia. Pennsylvania provides for gradual emancipation of slaves. Slavery abolished in Massachusetts.

1783 American Revolution ends in emancipation for the thirteen colonies, but not for the slaves. Some five thousand Negroes, slave and free, fought beside white men for American independence.

1784 Connecticut and Rhode Island adopt laws for gradual emancipation of slaves.

1785 New York abolition society formed.

1787 Free African Society founded. African Free School opens in New York City. Northwest Ordinance adopted by Congress, prohibiting slavery in the Northwest Territory.

1789 United States Constitution adopted, sanctioning and protecting slavery, without using the word. Representation was apportioned on a three-fifths basis for "other persons" (slaves), the slave trade was extended for twenty years, and provision made for the return of runaway slaves.

1790 757,208 Negroes in United States, 19.3 per cent of population. About 700,000 are slaves.

1791 Bill of Rights (first ten amendments to the Constitution) goes into effect. Benjamin Banneker, free Negro of Maryland, begins issuing his almanacs.

1793 Fugitive Slave Law adopted by Congress, strengthening extradition of slaves. Eli Whitney invents cotton gin, producing increased demand for Negro slaves.

1794 First convention of abolition societies meets in Philadelphia. Slave trade with foreign countries prohibited by Congress.

1796 Colored Methodist Episcopal Zion Church established in New York City.

1798 Georgia—last state to do so—abolishes slave trade.

1800 1,002,037 Negroes in the United States, 18.9 per cent of population. Gabriel Prosser's plan for mass slave rebellion in Virginia betrayed and slave leader hung.

1807 Congress prohibits the importation of slaves into the United States.

1810 1,377,508 Negroes in United States, 19 per cent of population.

1812 Free Negroes and slaves serve in War of 1812.

1816 African Methodist Episcopal Church founded in Philadelphia. American Colonization Society formed in Washington to resettle freed Negroes in Africa.

1817 Free Negroes meet in Bethel Church, Philadelphia, to oppose American Colonization Society.

1820 1,771,656 Negroes in United States, 18.4 per cent of population. Missouri Compromise adopted by Congress, prohibiting slavery in territory of Louisiana Purchase north of 36° 30', except Missouri, during territorial period. *The Emancipator,* published in Tennessee, is first abolitionist paper in the South. Congress declares foreign slave trade piracy, and punishable by death.

1821 Antislavery newspaper, *Genius of Universal Emancipation,* started by Benjamin Lundy in Ohio.

1822 Liberia founded on west coast of Africa, by freed Negroes, under the Colonization Society. Denmark Vesey, free Negro, leads slave revolt in Charleston, South Carolina.

1826 John B. Russwurm graduates from Bowdoin, first American Negro to receive a college degree.

1827 Russwurm and Samuel E. Cornish publish *Freedom's Journal,* first Negro newspaper in United States.

1829 David Walker, free Negro, publishes *Walker's Appeal,* calling on slaves to struggle militantly against bondage. George Horton, free Negro of North Carolina, publishes poems, *Hope of Liberty.*

1830 2,328,642 Negroes in United States, 18.1 per cent of population. Over two million are slaves. Negroes from seven states meet in Philadelphia to organize colored convention movement.

1831 William Lloyd Garrison establishes his abolitionist newspaper, *The Liberator,* in Boston. Nat Turner leads slave revolt in Southampton County, Virginia, is captured and executed. New repressive measures against the slave are adopted throughout the South.

1832 New England Anti-Slavery Society formed in Boston.

1833 American Anti-Slavery Society founded in Philadelphia. Female Anti-Slavery Society formed, with Lucretia Mott as president. John Greenleaf Whittier publishes his antislavery tract, *Justice and Expediency*. Great Britain abolishes slavery in her colonies. First antislavery book published: Lydia Maria Child's *Appeal in Favor of That Class of Americans Called Africans*. Oberlin, first coeducational college, opens doors to Negroes, too. Prudence Crandall forced to close school for Negro girls in Canterbury, Connecticut.

1834 Mobs riot against Negroes in New York City and Philadelphia.

1835 Mob violence against abolitionists and against schools for Negroes spreads. Garrison mobbed in Boston, Noyes Academy in New Hampshire wrecked, abolitionist mail seized and burned in Charleston, South Carolina.

1836 Abolitionists petition Congress to end slavery in the District of Columbia. Gag Rule adopted to table all abolition petitions.

1837 The Reverend Elijah P. Lovejoy, abolitionist editor, killed by proslavery mob in Alton, Illinois, while defending his press.

1838 Frederick Douglass escapes from slavery. *Mirror for Liberty,* first Negro magazine, launched by David Ruggles. Charles Lenox Remond, free Negro of Salem, Massachusetts, begins antislavery lecturing career. Joshua R. Giddings of Ohio is first abolitionist elected to Congress. Proslavery mob destroys Pennsylvania Hall in Philadelphia because of antislavery meetings held there.

1839 Samuel Ringgold Ward becomes agent for American Anti-Slavery Society. Abolitionists form Liberty Party at Amenia, New York. African slaves mutiny aboard the *Amistad,* are captured by United States warship. Supreme Court declares them free in 1841.

1840 2,873,648 Negroes in United States, 16.8 per cent of population. *National Anti-Slavery Standard* founded in New York City. James G. Birney, running for President on Liberty Party ticket, gets 7,069 votes.

1841 Douglass makes first antislavery speech in Nantucket. Becomes agent for New England Anti-Slavery Society. Slaves aboard the *Creole,* sailing from Virginia to New Orleans, revolt and force the ship to dock at Nassau in the Bahamas, where British court frees them. The Reverend James W. C. Pennington, graduate of Heidelberg, publishes *A Textbook of the Origin and History of the Colored People.*

1843 Henry Highland Garnet, at Negro convention in Buffalo, calls for armed resistance to slavery. William Wells Brown begins antislavery lecture career. Martin R. Delany starts newspaper, *The Mystery,* in Pittsburgh.

1844 Liberty Party candidate for President, James Birney, polls 60,000 votes.

1845 Texas annexed by United States, against vigorous opposition of abolitionists. Douglass lectures in Great Britain, publishes *Narrative of the Life of Frederick Douglass.*

1846 Mexican War begins, denounced by abolitionists as war to extend slavery.

1847 *North Star,* newspaper, edited by Frederick Douglass, begins publication in Rochester, New York.

1848 Free Soil Party formed of antislavery Democrats, Whigs, and Liberty Party men, gets 291,263 votes on a "Free soil, free speech, free labor, and free men" platform.

1849 Harriet Tubman escapes from slavery, later returns nineteen times to the South to bring out over three hundred slaves.

1850 3,638,808 Negroes in United States, 15.7 per cent of population. Compromise of 1850 adopted by Congress as formula to settle differences between North and South. It provides for no interference with slavery in District of Columbia, or with the interstate slave trade, and strengthens the Fugitive Slave Law. Many fugitives in the North flee to Canada for sanctuary. Mass resistance to the Fugitive Slave Law develops.

1851 In Boston, Shadrach, fugitive slave, is rescued from jail, and another fugitive, Thomas Sims, is returned to slavery. Jerry McHenry rescued from jail in Syracuse. At Christiana, Pennsylvania, armed free Negroes resist kidnappers and escape to Canada. Douglass turns to political action, joining the Liberty Party. Martin R. Delany enters Harvard Medical School.

1852 *Uncle Tom's Cabin,* Harriet Beecher Stowe's novel, published the previous year as a serial in the antislavery newspaper, the *National*

Era, appears in book form. Selling over a million copies in two years, and dramatized for stage, it has enormous influence. William C. Nell publishes a history, *Services of Colored Americans in the Wars 1776 and 1812.* Martin R. Delany publishes *The Condition, Elevation, Emigration, and Destiny of the Colored People of the United States.* John P. Hale, Free Soil candidate, receives 156,149 votes for President.

1853 National Council of Colored People formed in Rochester, New York. *Clotel, or The President's Daughter,* by William Wells Brown, first novel by an American Negro. *Narrative of Sojourner Truth, a Northern Slave.*

1854 Kansas-Nebraska Act repeals Missouri Compromise and permits admission of territories with or without slavery. Bloody struggle begins, to decide whether Kansas becomes slave or free state. Republican Party formed to oppose extension of slavery into the territories. Bostonians attack Federal courthouse in vain attempt to rescue Anthony Burns, arrested fugitive slave. Douglass lectures at Western Reserve on *Claims of the Negro Ethnologically Considered.* Lincoln University (originally Ashmun Institute) founded in Pennsylvania. Frances Harper publishes *Poems on Miscellaneous Subjects.*

1855 Douglass publishes *My Bondage and My Freedom,* Samuel R. Ward *The Autobiography of a Fugitive Slave,* and William C. Nell *The Colored Patriots of the American Revolution.*

1856 Wilberforce founded in Ohio as college for Negro youth. Republican candidate for President, John C. Frémont, runs second, receiving 1,335,264 votes, on a platform upholding Congressional authority to control slavery in the territories.

1857 Supreme Court decision on case of Negro Dred Scott holds Negroes "had no rights which the white man was bound to respect," and that they could not rightfully become citizens.

1858 Negro fugitive John Price is rescued from slavecatchers by Oberlin College students and a professor. William Wells Brown writes *The Escape,* first play by an American Negro.

1859 John Brown, with five Negroes among his men, seizes federal arsenal at Harpers Ferry in plan to strike a blow against slavery. Many of the men are killed; those captured are hung. *Anglo-American* magazine begins publication in New York City. The last slave ship, the *Clothilde,* arrives in Mobile Bay.

1860 4,441,830 Negroes in United States, 14.1 per cent of population. Four million are slaves. Abraham Lincoln, Republican Party candidate, elected President. South Carolina secedes from the Union.

1861 The Civil War begins. School for contrabands opens at Fortress Monroe, Virginia. Later it becomes Hampton Institute.

1862 Freedmen's Relief Association organized. Congress abolishes slavery in territories of the United States, and approves enlisting freed Negroes in the Army. The First South Carolina Volunteers, chiefly ex-slaves, organized as the first Negro regiment.

1863 Emancipation Proclamation goes into effect, declaring "forever free" all slaves in states still in rebellion against the United States.

1865 Lee surrenders at Appomattox and Civil War ends. Some 250,000 Negroes served in Union forces; 38,000 lost their lives. Lincoln assassinated and Andrew Johnson becomes President. Freedmen's Bureau established by Congress. Thirteenth Amendment to the Constitution adopted, abolishing slavery. Shaw, Atlanta, and Virginia Union colleges for Negroes founded in the South.

READING LIST

Aptheker, Herbert. *A Documentary History of the Negro People in the United States.* New York: Citadel, 1951.
Several hundred documents, dating from 1661 to 1910, are included in this book of almost 1,000 pages, the most comprehensive collection available.

Bontemps, Arna. *Story of the Negro.* New York: Knopf, 1951.
Against the background of history on a world scale are presented the stories of dozens of men and women who influenced the course of the struggle.

Botkin, B. A. *Lay My Burden Down.* Chicago: University of Chicago Press, 1945.
A folk history of life under slavery and after emancipation, collected from the memories of the survivors of those times.

Brown, Sterling A., Arthur P. Davis, and Ulysses Lee. *The Negro Caravan.* New York: Citadel, 1941.
This huge anthology of the writings of American Negroes includes short stories, poems, excerpts from novels and plays, folk literature, biography, autobiography, and essays. In the appendix is a valuable chronology that parallels events in the Negro world with the larger American scene.

Buckmaster, Henrietta. *Let My People Go.* New York: Harper, 1941.
A narrative of the Underground Railroad and the growth of the abolition movement, based on superb scholarship and told with dramatic power.

Filler, Louis. *The Crusade Against Slavery.* New York: Harper, 1960.
A thorough treatment of the abolitionist movement from 1830 to 1860, with its crosscurrents and personalities kept in clear perspective. It helps the reader see how the antislavery movement was related to the many reform movements of its generation.

Franklin, John Hope. *From Slavery to Freedom.* New York: Knopf, 1956.
The classic, most detailed one-volume history of American Negroes, by one of the best authorities.

Hughes, Langston, and Milton Meltzer. *A Pictorial History of the Negro in America.* New York: Crown, 1963.
Over 1,000 prints, drawings, paintings, cartoons, broadsides, posters, and photos are combined with a swift narrative in a panoramic history that comes down to today's headlines.

Litwack, Leon F. *North of Slavery.* Chicago: University of Chicago Press, 1961.
The second-class status of the Negro in the free states before the Civil War, a much-neglected subject, is thoroughly investigated.

Logan, Rayford W. *The Negro in the United States.* New York: Van Nostrand, 1957.
A handy, pocket-sized history by one of the leading historians of the Negro.

Quarles, Benjamin. *The Negro in the Civil War.* Boston: Little, Brown, 1953.
The record of the Negro in the armed forces and in service behind the lines, and his struggle to win equal treatment.

Redding, J. Saunders. *They Came in Chains.* Philadelphia: Lippincott, 1950.
A poetic and authoritative history of the American Negro.

Stampp, Kenneth M. *The Peculiar Institution.* New York: Knopf, 1956.
A close study of what southern slavery meant to the Negro and how he reacted to it, and the impact of bondage on the whole country.

Sterling, Dorothy. *Forever Free.* New York: Doubleday, 1963.
A brief and very readable chronicle of the Negro's fight for freedom, climaxing in the Emancipation Proclamation.

Index

ABOUT THE AUTHOR

MILTON MELTZER has long had a deep interest in social reform and its effects upon the American people. His previous books—*A Pictorial History of the Negro in America; Mark Twain Himself; Milestones to American Liberty; A Thoreau Profile; Thoreau: People, Principles, and Politics;* and *A Light in the Dark: The Life of Samuel Gridley Howe*—have all reflected his concern.

Mr. Meltzer attended Classical High School in Worcester, Massachusetts, where he was born, and Columbia University. He is the editor of a medical newspaper, and has written for magazines, newspapers, radio, television, and documentary films. He has traveled throughout the United States and Europe. Mr. Meltzer and his wife live in New York City. They have two daughters.